SPEAKRETS®

The 30 Best, Most Effective, *Most Overlooked* Marketing And Personal Branding Essentials

Ruth Sherman

"Speech Coach to The Stars"

Norsemen Books

Print Edition ISBN: 978-0-9937968-5-2
eBook Edition ISBN: 978-0-9937968-6-9

Original Design: Sarah Ancalmo
Photography by: Monica True

Printed in the United States of America
Published by Norsemen Books

*ATTENTION CORPORATIONS, UNIVERSITIES, COLLEGES AND PROFESSIONAL ORGANIZATIONS**: Quantity discounts are available on bulk purchases of this book for educational, gift purposes, or as premiums for increasing memberships. Special book covers or book excerpts can be created to fit specific needs. For more information, please contact Norsemen Books: info@norsemenbooks.com or 1-206-734-4950

Dedication

To my husband, Brad Olsen-Ecker, and our daughters, Britt and Lily, without whose love and humor I would not be where I am today.

SPEAKRETS®

Table of Contents

SPEAKRETS®

INTRODUCTION

Most of us believe we know how to speak to and communicate with other people; most of us are comfortable doing so every day. These skills rank high on the list of essentials we all need to get ahead. Yet, for some reason, when it comes to either interpersonal communication, or speaking in public, most of us fall down on the job. Why is this?

The answer, I believe, lies in the fact that we get virtually no training in these skills. We're just expected to *know* them. And, today, the plethora of online venues for communication have only complicated matters, keeping us glued to our desks, writing to each other, even when we're in the same room! And when it comes to public speaking, we are really at a disadvantage because not only is there little training available, we've been led to believe some people have it and some don't, and if you're one of the ones who don't, then you're just out of luck.

Nothing could be further from the truth, of course. Public speaking is much closer to performing, which is something many of us have yet to master. When you get out there to speak before a group, you are putting on a show, and you have the starring role. Once you begin to think about presenting in this new way, some new principles come to mind, like training, preparation, rehearsal, and — oh, yeah — stage fright.

So, we're faced with a choice: We can either just muddle through, hoping and praying that the critical interactions and presentations are few and far between, or we take charge and get the assistance and support we need to master these all-important skills.

That's where this book comes in.

Many prominent business executives, Hollywood celebrities, and other public figures face the same kinds of communication challenges that most of the rest of the world does: They want to have good business relationships and leave a good impression when they speak and appear in public, and they want what they say to be consistent with the way they look and sound when they're saying it.

Having worked with these talented people for over two decades, I'm proud to be able to say that I've helped many of them become better speakers and communicators and become adept at creating a favorable public impression. I've also learned what the most accomplished of them have in common, and I've been able to isolate a number of core principles that virtually all great communicators master. I've summarized them in this book; I call these principles SPEAKRETS®, because they so frequently go unnoticed, or at least unimplemented and unappreciated. If they aren't exactly secrets, they might as well be.

Effective speaking and communicating are the best marketing and personal branding tools that *no one wants to use*. To be specific, most people avoid implementing these core professional techniques, not because they are incapable of becoming good speakers, but because doing so requires a modest investment of time and practice. The fact is, though, that at some point in everyone's career, presenting and speaking, as well as masterful interpersonal communication, become necessities that only increase in frequency and importance as one advances. Those who abandon the opportunity to enhance their own latent ability to communicate powerfully, concisely, and persuasively are, in essence, abandoning their own careers and their own futures.

There is a piece of very good news here and it is this: It is never too late to learn to become a superb and confident communicator and a dynamic and effective speaker.

My SPEAKRETS® show you how.

PART ONE: PRIVATE SPEAKRETS®

Learn and practice these foundation principles on your own and join the family of powerful communicators.

SPEAKRETS®

SPEAKRET #1: Listen

-Ruth's Truth-

Listening is the most important – and most neglected – of all the persuasion and communication skills.

It comes as a surprise to many people to learn that listening is the essential, but too frequently overlooked, prerequisite to persuasive speaking.

There are few if any persuasive speakers who are not also good listeners. What does it mean to be a good listener? Consider the following true story. I was working with a CEO client a while back. I asked him how business was going. He threw up his hands in frustration and said it wasn't going at all well. Business was substantially down and the stock price was getting hammered. Then he asked, "What are you seeing?"

What Would You Have Said?

At that point, I could have given him a long monologue about what the last six months had been like for my business, but I didn't. This executive was not asking a question about how business was for me, but, knowing that I work for a wide range of industries, was asking what I was seeing generally in the marketplace. At that moment, because I was listening carefully, I recognized my client was looking for some insights and advice. I seized the opportunity.

During our subsequent discussion, I asked questions and listened to his responses. I shared my impressions. We eventually got to an area where there was some pain that my expertise could alleviate, and I freely shared my recommendations. I did not try to convert our talk into a contract. Instead, I asked directly and sincerely how I could help him. He responded by asking me for a favor, something I'd have to spend two to three (uncompensated) hours fulfilling. I was glad to do this, because I knew it would solidify our relationship. I didn't have to think twice.

Eventually, I got another assignment from him – all because I was willing to listen. In the vernacular of business, I closed the sale. This proves the larger point: All persuasion is rooted in the empathy of the listener.

Speaking to Persuade Means Understanding Needs

Listening is what happens when we open ourselves up to other people's perceptions of what they need. Speaking to persuade is impossible if you don't have any sense of what the person or people you are speaking to actually need!

Many people have the idea that listening is hard work, but that is untrue. Listening is actually relaxing and enjoyable. It's a good break from talking. It's also tremendously rewarding because of the opportunities it offers to learn. Listening to people is a marvelous way to find out things about them personally, about their universe, about their businesses, their lives and, of course, their needs, which they may not always be able to articulate. We're usually so distracted, however, by all the noise around us that we've become terrible at the skill.

Does your mind ever race to some other item on your to-do list when someone is talking to you?

When someone is speaking, do you ever find that you're already planning your response before the person has finished his or her point?

Do you answer the phone or accept other interruptions when someone is speaking to you?

Do you frequently interrupt the speaker?

Do you immediately forget the name of someone you've just been introduced to? (Me, too.)

The above are examples of hearing, but not listening; information goes in one ear and out the other. These behaviors are easy to change.

Great Listening is Empathetic and Intent

One of the most fundamental techniques of listening is empathy. Empathy is a primary interpersonal skill and a basic element of human moral development. It is the ability to identify with another's situation, feelings, and motives, to imagine what the person is experiencing or has experienced. It requires a willingness to extend oneself emotionally by summoning feelings. Empathetic, intent listening delivers the following benefits:

- *Builds self-esteem in the person who is being listened to.*

- *Encourages creative thinking.*

- *Bolsters your ability to gather information.*

- *Builds and nourishes relationships.*

- *Leads to questioning and clarifying.*

- *Heightens others' regard of the listener.*

- *Shows you care.*

- *Increases the impact of your later communications.*

Think about specific times someone has listened intently and empathetically to you - perhaps a boss, a friend, a doctor – and remember how satisfying it felt. The same thing will happen with your clients and customers when you start listening intently and empathetically to them.

Becoming an intent, empathetic listener takes presence, practice, discipline and patience. I'm always working on it. But you'll find if you take the time now to listen to your clients and customers and act as their trusted advisor, they will learn to depend on and turn to you to help them grow their businesses. Remember, it's YOU they are really buying!

SPEAKRETS® TOOLKIT
Steps to Becoming a Trusted Advisor By Listening

While poor listening can be changed, the change does not happen automatically. Some effort and technique must be applied. Here are some steps you can take right now to improve your one-on-one listening skills.

1. Ask your client or customer to share a meal, coffee or drink. Then have a conversation. Ask probing questions and listen carefully to the responses.

2. Give your full attention. Don't answer the phone or accept other interruptions.

3. Show your attention with both your body language and with vocal cues ("uh-huh," "I see," "yes," etc.).

4. Resist the urge to interrupt except to ask for clarification or check for understanding ("Let me be sure I understand you...").

5. Be self-disclosing; share just a little information about yourself that's not strictly necessary.

6. If your mind begins to wander, exercise discipline and bring it back. Ask your client to repeat anything you may have missed.

7. Don't take notes. Instead, when you leave your client or customer, take a few minutes to jot down the most salient points he or she raised. It's okay if you don't remember absolutely everything and you'll be surprised at what you do remember because you were (mostly) listening well.

SPEAKRET #2: Be Your Best Self

-Ruth's Truth-

Instead of striving for "authenticity," become the best, true version of yourself in each unique situation to captivate and touch people.

One of my kids is gay. I've been public about it since she gave me the go-ahead shortly after coming out when she was 14. That was in 2007.

I love my kids, equally, without reservation. Most parents do. In taking a public stand, however, I was afraid. Afraid of what people would think of me, afraid of drawing unwanted attention to my daughter, and, I'll tell you frankly, afraid of what it would mean for business. So even though I was comfortable talking with friends and family about it, I wasn't exactly shouting it from the rooftops.

In 2011, when the New York State Legislature was debating whether to allow gays to marry, I could be silent no longer. Although I am not a resident of New York, I did live there for many years and currently live in a nearby suburb. I conduct a lot of business there and feel as if I have a stake in it. I love the place. So does my family.

After the legislation passed, I decided to write a newsletter about how my family figured in it. My challenge was to make the business connection because that's what my readers count on me for. The hook was how being my best self would actually be good for business. The example I used was my daughter, who, to her eternal credit, is comfortable with who she is, has no trouble talking about it and advocating for herself, and has harnessed technology and social media. By being her best self, her true self, she has easily and organically attracted tens of thousands of followers.

As with everyone in business, attracting followers has been a goal of mine, too, but it has been neither easy, nor organic.

I was thrilled, therefore, when people responded to my newsletter in droves. Suddenly they felt they knew me a little better. My struggle was not identical to theirs, but similar and familiar. And here is something truly remarkable: Regardless of how they felt personally about the issue of gay marriage – and I know of several who had religious or political objections – they were universally kind and appreciative.

On the heels of that newsletter, I found a new freedom. After all, if I could let people in on something so deeply personal, I could let them in on other things, too. And by doing so, I have been able to connect more fully and extensively than I ever imagined.

We All Have Different Selves

When I'm coaching clients on public speaking or presentation, they often worry aloud to me that they don't want to come across as fake or phony. They often use the term, "inauthentic." My first response is that authenticity (or the current definition) is misunderstood. My second response is we each have many different selves. For instance, we're different with our bosses than we are with our peers; we're different with our friends than with our families; we're different with our kids than we are with our pets. And we're definitely different delivering a presentation than we are when we're speaking to a colleague in the corridor. The list goes on. We must be because each environment and situation demands it. Furthermore, we adapt to these environments and change our communication strategies without consciously thinking about it and, most of the time, without any training.

The fact that we have these different ways of being ourselves doesn't make us inauthentic. Quite the opposite: Our capacity to adapt and change our style of communication indicates a high level of knowledge and ability.

Finding Your Essence

Even with our adaptations, there is a common thread that is present in each: your core ethics and values. These don't change. They form the essence of who you are. And if you find they do fluctuate, then you must ponder that because it will stop you from achieving what you want to, from living your dream.

This aligns perfectly with what one of my coaches, the superb motivational speaker, Glenna Salsbury, counsels: For a person to be truly authentic, there has to be intention. The heart must be aligned with the message. And it doesn't matter if you say it out loud or not. Being settled on the inside, knowing your core ethics and values, are strongly felt by audiences, even if they aren't obvious or easy to observe.

Embracing your essence can be difficult, particularly if it isn't politically correct, or it's non-conforming. Once it is achieved, however, there is freedom and the task turns to coupling that essence with performance, regardless of the naysayers or objections. The resulting independence permits us to do our absolute best and arrive at a place where what we do feels easy and right. Fear takes a back seat, and we are able to take more risks. When our essence is clear and aligned with business, everything comes together, and there is a sense of inner peace and confidence in our communication that is magnetic. It's where charisma is born.

Beware: No amount of communication "technique" can mask a phony. And I say that without accusation. It's a hard thing to come to, especially when you're trying to make ends meet. Once you have established your best, true self with an audience (whether it is an audience of one or an audience of millions) you will have earned the right to be heard - and the right to persuade.

The clear sense that you know what you are doing, know why you are doing it, and are willing to express or project comfort with what you feel strongly about is what people respond to (and pay real money for). It is a necessary prerequisite of all effective business communication. Anything else risks disengagement by your clients and prospects. You know what I'm talking about. I've experienced it myself. While you won't attract everybody and will even repel some, the right people will appear.

Armed with your truth, you are ready to take a stand, challenge your audience, and establish irresistible "authenticity." Only then can truly powerful communication become possible.

SPEAKRETS® TOOLKIT

Start thinking:

1. What are your core ethics and values?

2. What is the one thing you are passionate about, yet afraid to take a public stand on?

SPEAKRETS®

SPEAKRET #3: Shatter The Charisma Myth

-Ruth's Truth-

Charisma isn't inborn. It's <u>learned</u>.

It's always fun to look at who gets labeled with that mysterious quality called "charisma" - and why. JFK had it; so did Ronald Reagan. Bill Clinton, too. Mitt Romney does not. Neither does Barack Obama – outside the big arenas.

So what is it about certain people that makes us gush?

First things first: There is a belief held by many people that charisma is inborn; supposedly, you either have it or you don't and if you don't then you are just out of luck. But that is wrong. It's a myth! Charisma is not inborn; it is learned.

Now it could be argued that some people are born with a personality type that gives them an edge in the charisma department. But if we look closely at what these folks are actually doing, we can break it down into discrete behaviors.

First, charismatic people ask good questions and listen carefully to the answers. They understand that people's favorite subject is – you guessed it – themselves! Everyone loves a good listener. (Speakret #1.) As the author and speaker Susan RoAne says, "You don't recommend your doctor by saying, 'You ought to go to my doctor. She doesn't listen to me.' "

Second, the charismatic among us really like people, find them fascinating and look forward to meeting them and building relationships with them. They are not faking it. They are genuinely, authentically interested in people, very focused on what they can give… not what they can get. This is a critical quality because it eliminates them as a threat, which, unfortunately, has infected so many business gatherings these days. (By the way, you can be shy and/or introverted and still be charismatic. See Speakret #20.)

Good In A Room

Third, the most important skill of charismatic people is they project a sense of personal comfort and inner confidence. We often hear that charismatic people are "comfortable in their own skin." That may or may not be true. We have no way of knowing for certain whether JFK, for example, was a content person, comfortable within himself and with his life. In fact, history now tells us he had significant personal problems. We KNOW Bill Clinton has issues. What people like Kennedy and Clinton are clearly able to do, however, is to project confidence. Even if they don't feel it.* This is a neat trick because there are many people who may not be outgoing by nature, but who know that when they walk into that crowded room, they must assume a particular bearing so they can leave a positive impression. They want their effort to be worthwhile. They don't want to waste their time by hanging out alone at the bar.

If I had to describe charisma simply, I would say this:

Charisma is the ability to draw others into your world and make them feel important.

It's about putting yourself in your conversation partner's shoes, having empathy. And, while I list some qualities the charismatic possess, I also want to mention the many things that are not necessary such as having a lot of money, fancy jewelry, an expensive car or a degree from an elite college.

Now, here's the good news: All the skills I describe above are available to anybody who wants to learn them. People who are identified as having charisma learned at some point during their lives that certain behaviors worked to their advantage and they could practice them and improve.

Not all business leaders have charisma, just like not all U.S. presidents or presidential candidates do. But here's the point: They could, and I think the world would be a more interesting place if they did.

*For those of you who may be confused when I say projecting confidence without feeling confidence is ok, or think this is exactly the opposite of being your best, true self (Speakret #2), they are not, in fact, mutually exclusive. By acting out your charisma, people will respond in kind and that feedback will have the magical effect of helping you feel it.

SPEAKRETS® TOOLKIT

Tune-up your charisma this week:

1. Project confidence and comfort (even if you don't *feel* it) by striding into a room and looking like you're glad to be there (even if you're not).

2. Introduce yourself to others with a smile and a firm handshake.

3. Ask people about themselves.

4. Lean in to listen to their answers to show interest and engagement.

5. Offer to connect people to others in your network.

6. At a table with 9 people you don't know? Act like a "host" instead of a "guest."

SPEAKRET #4: Words CAN Hurt

-Ruth's Truth-

Calibrate your communication with the twin goals of being clear and direct, while causing the least offense.

I had to manage a family business situation recently. Naturally, it was inherently laden with emotions that came at me from all directions including from the inside. In addition, I was forced to take on a role that meant having to speak some unpleasant truths to family members whom I love and respect in many ways, but who were not ready or open to hearing them. Furthermore, my partner in this leadership role had a weak communication style that left room for interpretation and, unfortunately, the interpretations being made were the wrong ones. Very uncomfortable. Still, the job had to get done and as a professional communicator, I knew what was needed to be sure everyone had the correct information with which to act.

Now, I'm not immune to hurtful and offensive language directed at me and even though I knew where it was coming from, when the first missile hit, I reacted very poorly, sending missiles right back. Even though my words were accurate, my angry and sarcastic tone made it impossible for the people to hear and make sense of them. Not productive at all because these individuals came back at me later on taking exactly the same position. I had failed.

Armed with the earlier experience, I was determined to succeed the second time. I set a goal to deliver the information in a manner where there would be no room for misinterpretation and limit the amount of hurt and offense my words would likely cause.

Here's what I considered as I calibrated my communication:

- *Doing what was best for the group and the business was my mandate and my responsibility.*

- *There were actions on the part of some that were affecting the business in deleterious ways that had to be stopped.*

- *I anticipated the ferocious and righteous anger some members of the group would have and practiced responding to their attacks and objections. (Speakret #29.)*

- *Peoples' feelings were important to me, but second to making sure they had accurate information, which I felt they deserved and could make good use of.*

- *I was very emotional myself about the whole business, so had to constantly check my reactions.*

I'd like to tell you that everyone came away happy, but that would be untrue. Although I attempted to reach out in a positive way, I was rebuffed. Could I have done better? Possibly, but I do know I did the best I could then and spent an awful lot of time trying. I am optimistic, however, with time, the hard feelings (on both sides) will dissipate.

The good news is that with some carefully planned tactics, I was able to reach my goals. They heard me, the bad actions stopped, and the business began moving along in a positive direction.

Think Before You Hit "Send"

We've all been there. Someone sends an email and the tone is aggressive or angry. Or, maybe you can't put your finger on it, but it seems off, somehow. If you're like most people (and me), your first reaction is to fire off a matching response. But that's usually a bad idea because things can really go south very quickly. Instead, it's best to stop and think before hitting the send button.

Words are, of course, primary and powerful. They can be positive vehicles of persuasion (Speakret #13). Or they can be forces for conflict and discord. If you have any doubt about that, take a tour of some of the blogging sites or YouTube to see some of the incredibly offensive things people say. Delicately defined as "snark," these online displays of anger, irritation and just plain gratuitous emotion have really gotten out of control. I call it "verbal violence."

At least when we're communicating in person, we have nonverbal communication to add meaning to our words, whether good or bad (Speakret #26). It's our current culture of distance communication through writing that has me worried because of its tremendous potential for miscommunication and the bad blood that often results.

Beware The Online Disinhibition Effect

What has resulted from our continuing preference for communicating via written means (email, text, social media) is a significantly lower level of inhibition and not in a good way. It is a developing concern among professionals in both the business and psychological realms.

Apparently, when we are communicating by these means, we are more likely to "flame" or express ourselves inappropriately. We more easily say things while sitting alone at the keyboard that we would never say face-to-face. These are the types of things we might even decide to let go, leave unmentioned or, at the very least, state more diplomatically. In fact, there is a technical name for this type of behavior: The online disinhibition effect, which refers to how we behave with less restraint in cyberspace.

I began to notice and write about this phenomenon a few years ago with my kids, who seemed able to be very frank with friends and others in their IM networks. At first, I admired that they could and would say what they really felt. I thought it was refreshing. As a regular cheerleader for honesty in communication, I could not imagine how this could be a bad thing - until one of them broke up with a boyfriend via text message. That was my wake-up call. For the important stuff, face-to-face has tremendous advantages. (I'm not saying that two 16-year-olds breaking up is that important; it is, however, practice for dealing with future conflicts.)

When we communicate facing another person, a cascade of nonverbal signals that can be very subtle constantly cues us. The flick of an eyebrow, the twitch of a mouth are only two among many other signs we read and consider. They occur in fractions of seconds and we are barely conscious of them, but we do read and consider them and they influence our responses. Our empathy centers are activated and we work to ensure the communication stays on track, even goes well.

And empathy is key. In my speeches and writings, I identify it as one of three critical communication skills. (The other two are apology and courtesy. Speakret #10). When we are alone, typing, there is an absence of information that we instinctively respond to when we are in another's presence. We hit send before we think better of it. This creates problems. I see it with my clients all the time and I experience it myself both in email exchanges and in rude and gratuitous comments to my blogs. It is a major component of cyber-bullying of young people.

It is just too easy to hit that send button. I know we live in a frenetic, sometimes frantic world, but it's important to take a step back. So follow this rule: If you wouldn't say it in person, don't say it in writing.

SPEAKRETS® TOOLKIT

Here are some of the techniques to use the right words in difficult situations:

1. Keep a calm voice.

2. Be clear and direct.

3. Avoid sarcasm or emotional language.

4. Allow others to react and respond emotionally.

5. Keep body language relaxed and laid back, leaning in only when you have something important to say.

6. Repeat and paraphrase when you notice they aren't getting it.

7. When you receive a rude or snarky email, don't hit "reply." Instead, hit "forward." Then respond in kind. Since no one's name will be in the "send to" area it will enable you to get it out of your system and give you time to reconsider.

SPEAKRET #5: Do Your Homework

-Ruth's Truth-

Preparation is the magic bullet to successful communication and presentation – and the biggest obstacle.

I cannot think of a better way to increase your status in your job, business or industry than becoming a skilled speaker and communicator. Yet standing (or sitting) in front of a group – or in front of a boss, investor, or colleague – and presenting a point of view or delivering information is a daunting prospect for all kinds of people ranging from beginners to seasoned CEOs. There is good reason for this. Most people do not get much, if any, training during their many years of school and few companies provide it to employees as part of their professional development programs. The ones that do usually don't provide enough depth.

This means that employees, business owners and even CEOs are too often left to their own devices at important points in their professional lives. The fact is that somewhere along the road, you will be asked to deliver a presentation.

So what does it really take to master these essential, professional skills? It all starts with preparation.

I can't stress enough how important saying it out loud is – again and again and again – and the place where even top pros get tripped up. The amount of time you spend on practice depends on the stakes and the level of formality. That, and giving yourself enough time to accomplish your task so it becomes second nature and the words come easily will eventually make you an accomplished communicator and presenter and give you the best chance of reaching your goals.

The great actor, Michael Caine, is supposed to have said: "Rehearsal is the work, performance is the relaxation."

I take that to heart and so should you.

SPEAKRETS® TOOLKIT

These tips are just a start:

1. What time of day will I be speaking: morning, afternoon, evening; before or during a meal?

2. What type of presentation will I be giving?

3. What is the occasion?

4. Will I be using visuals?

5. What is the venue going to be like?

6. How long will I be speaking?

7. Who is in the audience and what do they have in common?

8. What is the make-up of the audience? (Level, gender, professional specialty, background, education, age, etc.)

9. How many people will there be in the audience?

10. How much do they already know about my topic and how much more do they need to know?

And perhaps most important of all...

11. What do I want to accomplish?

Once you've answered those questions, you'll ready to take the following critical prep steps.

1. **Get to work right away.** Don't put it off. You need the time. Jot down everything. You can always edit later.

2. **Organize.** Start your outline.

3. **Time yourself & edit.** No one likes a speaker who goes past his or her time allotment.

4. **Rehearse**. This means saying it out loud. We're all eloquent in our own heads. Practice much more than you think you have to.

SPEAKRET #6: Your Attire Speaks Volumes

-Ruth's Truth-

Dress and adornment – all the sartorial choices we make – communicate a strong message before a word is uttered.

There is this young feminist movement called SlutWalk. How's that for direct communication? SlutWalk's focus is to let people know that no matter what a woman wears, it's not an invitation to sex. I agree with this in principle.

Now, I've spent my entire professional career studying things like the communicative power of dress and adornment, and how thoughtful we must be about the messages we send in this way. I'm also a rabid feminist. So my first thought was, do these young women understand that everything we wear, all the choices we make, communicate something? Do they want to have it both ways, i.e., to be able to dress as they want but NOT have their manner of dress send a message? Or, are they trying to change minds about a particular manner of dress, defuse it, do away with the term, "suggestive?"

My conclusion is they have a ways to go before minds will be changed.

Everything You Weren't Born Wearing

Every choice we make about our personal appearance – from the shoes we wear to the color of our hair – fits into the category of dress and adornment. As the young women of SlutWalk demonstrate, the issue is becoming more complex and confusing. I can remember a time when it was very clear what to wear to work: Men wore suits, usually blue with white shirts and a striped tie. Shoes were always polished and hair was always cropped and neat. Women, as always, had many more choices, but suits were de rigueur and the main choice they faced each day was whether to wear a skirt or pants.

I like clothes. I think of them as a kind of art. When I step into a room, the way I'm dressed and adorned is the first thing people notice. What else is there? I haven't yet opened my mouth to speak. Therefore, I want what I'm wearing to say something about me and who I am. Clothing and accessories send messages, and choosing the right dress and adornment is an extremely important (and commonly overlooked) communication skill. If we're smart, we can use our clothing choices to send only the messages we want to send.

Chief among these messages is that we fit in – that we belong. Not long ago, I read an article about a particularly well-dressed businessman who travels internationally; he wears pocket squares in London but doesn't wear an overcoat in Paris, where men don't wear them. In New York, he ties his scarf one way and in Italy, he ties the same scarf in another way, all so as not to be seen as an outsider. The aim is to eliminate distractions.

Today, choosing what to wear varies widely from workplace to workplace, from location to location, and from situation to situation. Businesses want the clothes their employees wear to reflect the company values and services. For example, the creative fields (PR, advertising, publishing) have always allowed workers to dress a bit less formally and a bit more stylishly (artistically) than workers in other fields. Such fashion choices tell tells clients that the company is daring, willing to test limits, and unconventional. This is what clients expect and want from the work of such "creatives."

Investment bankers' choices tend to skew conservative. Even on "casual days," the choices are limited to khaki pants and a button-down shirt for men and skirts or slacks and sweaters for women. This type of dress says "safe" or "stable" – which is just how clients would like to be able to describe their investments. A similar dress code applies to attorneys, with the key word this time being "trust."

Technology or start-up type workplaces have yet a different sensibility, one that might be described as "surface appearance doesn't matter; it either works or it doesn't." Torn T-shirts, jeans, and casual grooming are all acceptable, even expected. Of course, that's mainly the engineers and programmers. This type of style communicates a certain set of values: Intelligent, even cerebral, and unconcerned with those surface issues. Even at a technology company, however, anyone who has to call on clients has some decisions to make. Can you show up for a high level meeting with the CIO at a major accounting firm wearing the types of clothing I described above? I don't think so.

Then we get to leadership dress. To look like a leader – which means to be seen as such both internally and externally – requires a certain careful, polished style. Every business leader I know – man or woman – is well dressed. This isn't cheap, but it is an essential prerequisite to effective communication within their chosen role. Dress and adornment send certain important signals that we expect to see from our leaders: Ready for serious business, strength, and an impression of financial success.

Here's the bottom line: We make a statement whenever we walk into a room, before we utter a word. That statement can take many forms, some of which are complementary to the message we want to deliver, and some of which conflict with that message.

Is the statement we are making with our dress and adornment consistent with our professional status, knowledge, and authority or does it send a message that has people thinking something else entirely?

This is the big hurdle the women of SlutWalk have to get over. I wish them luck.

SPEAKRETS® TOOLKIT

What do you communicate by what you wear?

Occasion	Outfit description	Message Sent?	Does it work?	If no, what changes?
Work?				
Casual office day?				
Social event daytime?				
Social event evening?				

SPEAKRETS®

SPEAKRET #7: Emblems Display Our Status

-Ruth's Truth-

The public evaluates us by things we use to decorate ourselves.

I was driving around my neighborhood, which happens to be in one of those upscale places where there are a lot of nice cars. I stopped at the local ice cream place, got out, and noticed an unusual car parked on the street in front of me. My husband pointed out that it was a Bentley – and not only a Bentley, but the Continental GT, a particularly sporty version of that venerable brand. Apparently it's the least expensive of the Bentley line, priced as of this writing at just under $200,000.00.

We also see the occasional Ferrari or Maserati from time to time, usually during the summer; these are only rarely parked in public, and even more expensive than the Bentley. On any given day, there are loads of BMWs and Mercedes parked all over the place. Almost every other car that I haven't mentioned so far is late model and nice-looking.

These cars are emblems we use to delineate and display our status to others, without showing our bank account. Status messages show up not just in the car, but also where and even if the car gets parked. These decisions mark the owner as someone who is of such means that a scratch, ding or dent is no big deal.

Cars are not the only emblems that affect one's perceived status and credibility; clothes and accessories serve this purpose, too. For women, the latest "it" bag or Jimmy Choos or Manolos serve as emblems. Sometimes the emblem is jewelry. A popular emblem for some men might be a wristwatch, which, at a certain level, must be Swiss. Generally speaking, big status is conveyed by big jewels or "bling" (I call them "headlights"), which can be worn by both men and women, though often it's the woman wearing the jewels and the man wearing the woman! I suppose there are plenty of "vice-versa" situations these days.

Emblems don't have to be expensive; some relatively cheap ones can say a lot about us. Think of what you conclude, more or less automatically, about someone who displays the latest iPhone or other technology. (Can't wait to see what happens with the Apple Watch.) What about computers? Are you a Windows or a Mac? As a long-time Mac user, I can clearly remember a time when people who used Macs were viewed as somehow lower-status, less technologically savvy, not to be taken seriously, more feminine (a negative connotation) than those who tussled with Windows. Hmm … sometimes perceptions about our emblems change (as we Mac fans knew they would).

The beautiful thing about emblems is that we get to choose them for ourselves.

In my case, cars don't do it for me, and they're not my emblems of choice. I drive a plain-vanilla Toyota Camry with a 4-cylinder engine, comfy, reliable and decent on gas. My engagement ring still has the small diamond that my husband could afford at the time. (But, when I move in certain circles, I secretly wish I had a bigger one.)

I do splurge on clothes, though, because I've found it sends a powerful message to prospects and clients. I love Italian and French designers and their tailoring. I also love smart, close-fitting clothes that have an edge. I consider them art. My wardrobe has staying power. What messages do these clothing choices send about me? Smart, chic, sophisticated, together and, of course, successful.

SPEAKRETS® TOOLKIT

What are your emblems of success and what messages are your emblems supposed to send to your audience about who you are, what you know, and how seriously you should be taken?

Emblem	Message Sent?	Consistent with your brand?	If no, what substitutions?
Car?			
Office décor?			
Watch?			
Smartphone?			
Computer (Mac or PC)?			
Dress & Adornment?			
Other Emblems?			

SPEAKRET #8: Seduce With Your Voice

-Ruth's Truth-

A beautiful speaking voice coupled with precise diction is like a fingerprint, a unique differentiator.

Many of my clients comment positively on my voice. They ask: "How can I get a voice like yours?" "Twenty years of voice training," is my usual glib reply.

You don't actually have to wait two decades to dramatically improve your speaking voice. I believe anyone can improve the quality of her or his voice in a matter of weeks. The key is practice.

Early on in my career, I recognized that a melodious, expressive voice and careful articulation could make a real difference in whether – and how attentively – people listened to me. I began to make a habit of listening to all the people whose voices I thought were great, and I tried to figure out what it was about those voices that appealed to me.

Three things, I realized, usually made an instant positive impression on me as a listener: Tone, vocal variety, and rhythm.

Tone

Good tone is a continuous, round, full, reverberating, musical sound. The voice with good tone fills all the space. James Earl Jones and the elegant news personality Diane Sawyer are classic examples of high quality tone. Barack Obama, when he's trying, has a pleasing instrument he knows how to play. Listen to Rush Limbaugh's voice (whether or not you like him), because it is definitely one of the things that makes him so successful. Radio personalities - DJs, talk program hosts, news reporters - usually have high quality voices because of the nature of the medium.

Developing a strong, resonant vocal tone is like building muscles in other parts of your body. You have to work out in order to build flexibility and strength.

Breath is the Life Of Your Voice

One extremely important part of the vocal machinery that generates good tone is our breathing mechanism, referred to in professional circles as the diaphragm. The diaphragm is a large muscle located directly under the lungs. It pulls air into the lungs and pushes it out.

Vocal Variety

This refers to how we use expression or vocal dynamics — highs and lows of pitch and volume — to give our words meaning. For example, a simple declarative sentence can have several meanings depending on which word is stressed…

"I'm **very** happy to meet you."

has a different meaning than…

"I'm very happy to meet **you**!"

Kill The Corporate Monotone

To make the most of your vocal variety, you have to be willing to ham it up and experiment. Many people have developed what I call the "corporate monotone." This is a flat vocal affect that sounds disconnected and disengaged.

Corporate settings are designed to squeeze all the emotion out of the workplace and the speaking voice hasn't been spared. This is unfortunate because what we've ended up with is a population of workers who cannot display any feelings with their voices. They speak in hushed, monotonous tones. They sound, frankly, bored, and to the listener, boring. This monotony impedes their ability to sell and business is all about selling, whether products, services or a point of view.

A great way to see how a different form of vocal expression can change perceptions for the better is to experiment with your outgoing voice mail messages.

Avoid using the boilerplate script; everyone knows to wait for the tone and to leave a detailed message. Instead speak simply and briefly in a warm and inviting way. You'll be amazed at the positive reaction.

Another terrific method of working on vocal variety is reciting a good, dramatic monologue. Something from Shakespeare such as the "Friends, Romans, Countrymen..." speech from Julius Caesar is a great choice, but virtually any theatrical or dramatic monologue that you like will do.

Finally, I often have clients read aloud from the newspaper as if they were anchoring the evening news.

Rhythm

When it comes to the speaking voice, rhythm refers to all the percussive aspects of speech including diction, articulation, accents, dialects, rate, pace, pauses, and silence.

Crisp up Your Diction

Diction, pronunciation, articulation, enunciation… they all have a similar meaning. Some speakers simply have poor diction habits. Slowing down is one simple way to improve diction. This basic technique seems to work miracles, because it allows the tongue and facial muscles to take more time and thus gain more precision. In particular, diction can be improved by paying attention to words ending in the sounds "t", "s" and "k." (I do not restrict sounds to the aforementioned letters, but rather the sounds dictated by these and other spellings.)

Bad diction is simply a bad habit. Once you start changing your habit to be more precise, you'll notice people leaning in, paying closer attention and isn't that worth a little work?

Accent or Dialect? Adapt, Don't Adopt

Accents and dialects cause people problems. For our purposes here, accents refer to the way non-native speakers of a given language speak it, applying the rules of their native language to a new language. Dialects refer to the regional differences of native speakers. So, people from Boston speak English differently than people from Los Angeles, even though both are native speakers. Then there is American English versus, say, Caribbean English, all native speakers applying different rules of pronunciation, variety, and rhythm.

Accents and dialects can be terrific differentiators, provided they are done well. That means the speaker must be comprehensible. The minute a listener has to take a moment to translate or understand is the minute you've lost them. To prevent your accent or regional dialect from becoming a distraction, you will have to slow down. You'll also have to tune in to your listeners' non-verbals. Are they engaged or are they nodding off? The key is to adapt.

As a native of the New York Metropolitan area, I know I speak fast. In fact, around here we judge people on their intelligence by how fast they speak – not that it's right! So, when I go to Mississippi to speak, where every day business speech is slower-paced and more relaxed, I have to adapt. Because of my musical ear, I always run the risk of taking on an accent, so I resist the strong tendency to adopt, which would not be authentic. Instead, I carefully listen and slow down, adapting just enough to make a connection.

Silence Speaks Loudly

We don't like silence. It scares us.   But it's a very effective technique to demonstrate confidence and command. A typical mistake is when presenters talk as they're changing slides. I always counsel them to be quiet as they move to the next slide. This is enormously difficult to do! However, it shows a high level of confidence.

Other places to pause include when you ask a question. Pause and wait for a response. State an interesting statistic. Pause to let people take it in. One way I've been using pausing and silence lately is when I do a presentation on the explosion of video. My opening statement is, "4 Plus Billion YouTube views per day!" Then I just shut up. The looks on people's faces indicate they are trying to wrap their heads around that number and what it means for them.

A beautiful speaking voice, with precise diction, accompanied by the strategic use of pauses and silences is like a fingerprint, a unique differentiator, a way to persuade and, yes, seduce your audiences. It always gets noticed. And since we're all professional voice users in one way or another, best to start internalizing that reality.

SPEAKRETS® TOOLKIT

The following is an exercise designed to demonstrate proper breathing with the diaphragm. It's also a great vocal warm-up:

1. Picture how you breathe after strenuous exercise. You chest heaves and you pant rapidly. (Or do a deep sigh.)

2. Bring your hands to the level of the bottom of your rib cage. Position them so they are directly one over the other, palms facing, elbows out to the sides.

3. Hook your fingers (minus the thumbs) together and pull but do not let go. You should feel the pull in your shoulders and upper chest wall. As you pull, take two or three deep breaths very slowly and look down. You should see your abdomen expanding and contracting. Keep your shoulders steady. Do not allow them to rise with each breath.

4. Now, take a deep breath and exhale, this time saying "ah...." and stay on it for 5 seconds. Repeat and hold it for 10 seconds, then 15. Finally, breathe and say "ah" for as long as you can. You should feel a strong contraction in your abdomen as you run out of breath. Relax your body and stretch.

5. Re-connect your hands and pull. Now, beginning at a middle pitch, take a deep, abdominal breath and say, "one," moving lower in pitch over about 5 seconds until your voice is very low. It should be a strong vocal sound. Do the same with two, three, four and five. Breathe before each one.

6. This time, count from one to five, without taking breaths, starting on a mid-level pitch with each number and heading lower, only move more quickly so that you are on each number for about 1-1/2 seconds.

7. Next, say the word "yum." Now, beginning at a very high pitch (falsetto), say "Yum, yum, yum, yum," repeating the phrase. Until you find yourself getting down very low. The "Y" and "M" in this word help to assure good voice placement. This means resonance and fullness without vocal strain. Do this a few times. You should feel the vibration of the sound in your sinuses. (This exercise is especially effective after a good meal.)

To begin mastering diction, try the following exercise:

1. Slowly say the words "tick-tock," "tick-tock," "tick-tock." Make sure you really pronounce your t and k sounds. There should be a strong puff of air expelled with each sound. Repeat a few times.

2. Now, say "ticketa-tocketa," "ticketa-tocketa," "ticketa-tocketa." DO NOT SUBSTITUTE A D SOUND FOR THE SECOND T. The pronunciation of these words should make active use of the tongue and teeth and sound very crisp. Repeat a few times.

SPEAKRET #9: Name-Calling Is An Art

-Ruth's Truth-

Foster good will by at least attempting to correctly pronounce an unfamiliar or foreign name.

When my oldest daughter, Britt, was applying to college, the first one to send her information addressed it to Butt. Yep, Butt. Can you imagine what that did to a 16-year-old's day? She did not attend that college.

Getting people's names right – or at least attempting to do so – can create huge amounts of good will. Even if the name is unfamiliar or difficult to pronounce or if you try, but get it wrong.

Cheek-SENT-me-high. Can you say that?

You would have to if you were lucky enough to meet Mihaly Csikszentmihalyi, the well-known creator of the "flow" theory of adult learning and achievement. His theory has nothing to do with pronunciation (but Google him anyway, because his work is fascinating). Establishing rapport with Csikszentmihalyi, however, would have a lot to do with pronunciation.

Imagine meeting the esteemed Dr. Csikszentmihalyi at an event. He introduces himself and hands you a business card. You try to make sense of that intriguing name. The way he says it seems to bear no relation to the way it's spelled. What do you do? Read on!

I am devoting an entire Speakret to the often-overlooked topic of name pronunciation because though the vast array of communications technologies at our disposal has produced some tremendous benefits, it has also taken some essential things away. For instance, in comparison with generations who preceded us, we have gotten out of practice at, and become unconcerned about, pronouncing proper nouns. (Proper nouns, of course, are the names of people, places and things; they are always capitalized.)

The research on pronunciation's value is clear. First and foremost, good pronunciation and clear speech facilitates communication. Pronouncing a name or place correctly demonstrates respect. The best communicators show this respect; they also make others feel important. Proper pronunciation furthers that goal. Showing you care about people is another worthy objective that is supported by correct pronunciation.

Finally, precise pronunciation makes a person sound intelligent, educated and worldly. Not a small thing in our global economy!

Begin With People's Names

Phonetics and syllable stress (syllable accents) are no longer a formal part of most schools' language arts curricula, and haven't been for years. Fortunately, we do not need formal training to effectively use the principles behind these techniques. The trick to pronouncing any unfamiliar word or name lies in finding sounds that do make sense to your eye and ear, substituting them for the letters and/or combinations of letters in the name, and then physically writing the phonetic pronunciation down in a way that helps you to make the correct sounds and stress the correct syllables. (Many database apps even contain a spot within each contact for the phonetic spelling of their names. Regardless, you can still add a phonetic spelling in an empty field.)

For example, Asian names are often quite difficult for English speakers to make sense of and pronounce. Sounds that are common in English simply do not exist these languages (and vice versa). One big difference is the pronunciation of the R and L sounds. Asian languages contain a sound that is a blend of the two, which is why we never know which sound to use and why native Japanese and other Asian speakers often have difficulty when pronouncing so many common English words. Then there's the question of how to stress the syllables within a given proper noun. We naturally follow English rules of syllable stress, but every foreign language has its own rules, some of them quite different from those followed in English.

Consider these Japanese names:

Naoko
Incorrect: Nay - OH - ko;
More correct: NAH-oh-ko

Takashi
Incorrect: tuh - KAH - shee;
More correct: TAH - kuh - shee

Do enough of these, and you will learn that syllable stress in 3-syllable Japanese names most often falls on the first syllable, not the second as is habit for English speakers following the rules of western languages. Syllable stress alone is often enough to bring about positive results.

Eastern European names, with their unfamiliar spellings, can be just as tricky. Take these Polish surnames:

Piotrowski
Incorrect: Pee-oh-TROW-skee;

More correct: Pyuh-TRAHV-skee

Wasikowska
Incorrect: Wah-sih-COW-ska;
More correct: Vah-shi-KOV-skuh

Practice Polish surnames enough and you might deduce that W sounds like V and the CZ combination sounds like CH (as in change).

Practice helps but you could also take a page from Whoopi Goldberg who has said the only way she got Iranian President Ahmadinejad's name right is by thinking of it as "Ahm-a-DINNA-jacket." Whatever works!

The Internet can also be helpful if you're looking to pronounce an unfamiliar name correctly including phonetic spellings and even audios. If you're stumped, do a search.

Ask For Help

What about social situations where it's impractical go to a website for aid? (Smartphones basically put the lie to that!) The best source of pronunciation help is the person whose name you're trying to learn. If you don't get it the first time, don't hesitate to ask the person to say it again, slowly. Assuming that business cards have been exchanged, try to jot down a phonetic pronunciation on the card. I promise you the person will not take offense, and may even be honored by your efforts. (Most people, after all, don't make the effort.)

If the tables are turned and you happen to have a name that you know is unfamiliar to your listeners - when you're traveling in a non-English speaking country, for instance - you can help your conversation partners by slowing down and giving them some tips on how to pronounce it. You may think of "Ruth" as a simple name, but when I was traveling in the Middle East recently, I always tried to help people with it. In Arabic, the R is rolled and the TH sound is nonexistent, leaving only the U, which is pronounced differently! I found that discussions about name pronunciation could actually be fun and a great cross-cultural conversation starter.

By the way, don't worry about your accent; it is unlikely you will ever sound like a native speaker of a language you did not grow up learning. Your efforts, however, will have a subtle, but powerful effect and be handsomely rewarded.

SPEAKRETS® TOOLKIT

Create a space in your contact manager/database to insert phonetic spellings for unfamiliar or difficult-to-pronounce names.

SPEAKRET #10: Know When to Say "Sorry!"

-Ruth's Truth-

Apology and expressions of regret are unsurpassed communication tools that will defuse any conflict.

During the past two presidential campaigns, when I was being called upon by the press to comment on the candidates' communication styles, I was asked by Lester Holt of MSNBC for one suggestion that would help each candidate improve. I said that John Kerry should tell more stories, because when he did that, it made him seem less wooden and more relatable. For President Bush, I suggested that he find a mistake he would be willing to own up to and apologize for.

At the time, it seemed that it had been a long time since anyone in any position of power had apologized for anything. The American public felt that some words of contrition from both its political and business leaders were long overdue. It seemed that no one was willing to step up, look people in the eye, and say, "I'm sorry." This is an issue we, as a society, still grapple with.

In my speeches and presentations on effective communication, I declare authentic and appropriate personal apology as one of the most powerful, persuasive communication tools. Unfortunately, I have to caution my audiences not to look to our business and political leaders as role models on this score. This is too bad, because not only is apologizing is a critical social skill, it is also a leadership skill that can be remarkably effective, regardless of what position you hold.

When a mistake is made or a personal wrong is committed, the resulting feelings can include anger, hurt, and/or betrayal. All of these reactions result in diminished trust. The hard work of building solid relationships is derailed. People who are mad at each other have difficulty working together. Naturally, business suffers. A well-timed and sincerely intended apology, however, can defuse such a situation almost instantaneously.

Most of us can empathize with a colleague who has made a mistake. We have a natural tendency to think, "There, but for the grace of God, go I." If an attempt is made at apology, we understand the humbling nature of the act and we feel for the apologizer. In addition, we realize that it often takes courage to admit a mistake, and that there is inherent risk to doing so. As a result, there may even be feelings of admiration that kick in for the person who apologizes. During the apology process, the power dynamics of the communication are effectively reversed. The person who felt victimized is now in the position of power and is given a choice to accept the apology and move on - or not.

For an apology to have maximum impact, timing is crucial. Another way to put this is: Don't put off an important apology! Get right to it and don't let things fester.

Apologizing alone is not enough. You must also have some solutions ready. In fact, I usually link apologizing with explaining. This does not mean creating excuses; it means proving that you have thought through the problem and have attempted to understand where things went awry and how to avert such situations in the future. The goal is for a conversation to take place with the give and take necessary to ensure understanding of all these points.

There's another important precondition: You have to mean what you say.

Many people ask me what to do when the situation in question is not their fault. Every situation is different, of course, but my advice is to not spend time and energy worrying about whose fault the problem really is. My own rule is that if by apologizing I can get things back on track, I do it. I apologize anyway. It's usually not a question of fault, but rather of keeping the lines of communication open and the relationship running smoothly. If it's the word "apology" itself that rankles, I often suggest substituting the word "regret" for "sorry."

It's a less emotionally charged word, and although it doesn't have quite the same impact, it may do the trick.

With a few notable exceptions, business leaders and politicians don't seem to be racing to apologize for the mistakes they've made in recent years. But that doesn't mean you can't.

Yes, it's hard. Yes, it's threatening. Yes, it works.

SPEAKRETS® TOOLKIT

The next time things go south either in your personal or business relationships, think about apologizing or expressing regret to get them back on track.

SPEAKRETS®

PART TWO: BUSINESS SPEAKRETS®

These principles will enable you to navigate the complex world of business interpersonal and speech communication from the inside out.

SPEAKRET #11: Know Your Audience

-Ruth's Truth-

If you don't know your audience, you won't be able to give them what they came for.

What was Priceline.com co-founder Scott Case doing speaking at Greenwich (CT) High School's commencement? It so happens Case is a Greenwich High School alum and obvious success story. On June 29, 2010, he returned to where it all began to impart words of wisdom to my daughter, Lily, and 690 of her fellow graduating seniors.

The location was the school's massive football field, students sitting in rows on the field, parents and others in the bleachers. The ceremony followed a typical route with speakers exhorting students to "do good," and "find work they love" – boring, boilerplate stuff. The kids just sat there. The adults just sat there, too. So, none of us were quite prepared for what came next. The class president who introduced Case gave us the first hint, mentioning during his intro that though they knew he was in somewhere on the school grounds, they didn't know exactly *where* Case was sitting or *what* he had planned. Clearly, he wanted it that way.

The introduction was made and from the audience, a figure with a red cap and gown - indistinguishable from the senior boys - stood up from among the nearly 700. Wireless microphone in hand, Case spoke as he made his way to the front of the audience area and ascended to the stage.

You could hear a pin drop.

Suddenly, what had been a humdrum, garden-variety high school commencement got game. Literally. A tradition of tossing around beach balls that administrators have for years unsuccessfully tried to discourage was instead *encouraged* by Case. So was the equally hated student tradition of blowing bubbles.

Already an accomplished entrepreneur and at the time the CEO and Chairman of non-profit, *Malaria No More*, he did not talk about himself. Oh no. He knew his audience. Not the parents. The graduates. He told them that though they might be concerned about their future, in fact, they'd already won the lottery:

- *They lived in the USA*

- *They had an education*

- *They were loved and had been taught life's basics*

Then, he asked them how many of them had cell phones on them and up went almost every hand – holding those phones. The administrators and many of the parents were chagrined, but not Case. He told them to text a nice message to the people that loved them.

Complete silence. From everyone.

He spoke a little while longer, encouraging the grads to make the most of what they'd been given and then he hit them with the BIG CLOSE: *Under every one of the 690 chairs was an actual lottery ticket.*

Wow.

And in that 15 minutes, by showing instead of telling, Scott Case taught these young people some other, valuable, albeit indirect lessons about knowing a diverse audience, capturing its attention, and keeping it in the palm of one's hand...

By the way, Lily won $27. A great start, don't you agree?

SPEAKRETS® TOOLKIT

- *Show, don't tell.*

- *Do the unexpected.*

- *Keep it short.*

- *Close BIG.*

SPEAKRET #12: Be A Super-Connector

-Ruth's Truth-

Introduce people to each other imaginatively and actively. You will be appreciated and remembered.

Some years ago, I received regular invitations to attend something called "China Dinners," the brainchild of one of my clients, a native of that country, lawyer and business executive. Early on in our relationship, we had great, long conversations about the importance of building relationships and effective self-marketing and I loved being filled in on cultural differences between the U.S. and China. One thing that is common to both (all) cultures, however, is the love of food and rich, intellectual conversations.

This client is what I would call a "Super-Connector." It's a level above being a connector, which is because it is done with an enormous amount of purpose and energy. There is constant thinking behind who in his network would benefit from knowing another member of that network.

These China Dinners were fashioned on the salons of the early 19th and 20th centuries. Salons originated as a periodic gathering of people of particular social and intellectual distinction. They've always been around, of course. At these dinners, which were held in a New York restaurant, there was always a wide range of expertise. In addition to the client, there would be journalists, consultants, small business owners, investment bankers and federal regulators. And me. The nationalities were generally representative of Asia (including other Asian countries) and the U.S. Ages ranged from the 20s to the 50s.

The discussion topics were equally extensive as well as provocative. We covered everything from the future of China (economic powerhouse certainly, eventual democracy maybe?) to the latest business news from that part of the world and how the globalization of trade affects everything. During one dinner, I led a discussion on the vital importance of good communication as a precursor to and indicator of success, especially at the senior executive level and absolutely critical in high-stakes situations. I also got to brag about my involvement in a film by a famous director of Chinese descent, which happened to be a Chinese language espionage thriller (with English subtitles) that takes place in China during World War II. As a result, I learned about other great Asian films and directors. Needless to say, the conversation was dynamic and fascinating.

What was particularly interesting is the way my client set it up. He would send the invitation about a week in advance with the list of guests who have confirmed. About 2 days before, he confirmed the dinner with an updated guest list and included links to several news articles concerning the discussion topic. He also mentioned some of the guests' areas of expertise so the invitees could all do a little research beforehand. This truly facilitated the conversation.

"Super-Connectors" are in an enviable position. People gravitate toward them and as along as we're talking about gravity, let's include the word, magnetic. And salons are a terrific method of helping identify you as a "Super-Connector" (as opposed to just a "connector"). What a great way to attract new and interesting people whom you would not ordinarily meet and whom you can add to your network. And being the organizer or host is such a great way to shine.

SPEAKRETS® TOOLKIT

Put together your own version of a "China Dinner."

Name of dinner:

Date:

Location:

Topic:

Invitees (limit to 8):

News articles/links on topic:

Send reminders/confirm guests:

    One week out:

    Two days out:

Eat, discuss, enjoy!

SPEAKRET #13: Persuasive Language - A Page From The Pros

-Ruth's Truth-

Words, carefully selected, can change hearts and minds.

If the campaign ads and stump speeches that take place every election cycle teach us anything about communication, it's this: When you're trying to persuade people to take action, identify a simple, powerful message and return to it as many times, and as emotionally as you possibly can.

In the trade, of course, this is known as "staying on message," and it's the first commandment of a successful campaign. Business communicators, alas, often ignore this valuable rule from the world of politics.

Here is the incredibly successful messaging the Republican Party has been using for many years (the "long period of time" component):

"Government is too big, spending is out of control and taxes must be cut."

It is simple (short, easy to remember), relevant (people are earning less and expenses are rising), and the emotional component is clear (everyone's emotional about taxes).

Another component is the discipline with which the message is disseminated: Virtually all Republican candidates and office-holders are united by it; they speak with one voice. Most people would be hard pressed to remember a time when that theme was <u>not</u> the Republican message. It's pure messaging mastery, with its power and success undeniable.

Businesses have been masterful with language, too, and below are some examples that are the stuff of legend:

- *"Don't leave home without it."* *(American Express)*

- *"Like a good neighbor, State Farm is there."*

- *"A diamond is forever."* *(DeBeers)*

- *"You're in good hands with All State."*

- *"Got Milk?"*

- *"They're GREAT!"* *(Kellogg's)*

So if your job is to persuade people to take action, start thinking about words. Throw some up on a flip chart or white board. Be outrageous and use really potent, emotionally laden words. I like to make two columns with nouns in the right-hand column and adjectives in the left-hand column. Then shuffle them around, trying out combinations and seeing which ones fit. Eventually, you'll come up with a phrase that resonates. Test it on your colleagues and friends.

Don't Change Your Message Too Soon

Once you've nailed it, guard against getting bored by it. (WARNING: You *will* get bored. This is a true hazard because it causes people to change their hard-won language before it's been around long enough to have an impact.) Then, repeat, repeat, repeat. Put it on all your branding. Say it to others constantly so it just rolls off your tongue. Eventually, people *will* buy your stuff (or your ideas).

Whether you agree with a particular political or business message or not, having the discipline to stay with it works! The persistence, passion and the discipline with which the GOP and the big business advertisers have spread their winning messages are admirable – and enormously effective.

P.S.: To all the Democrats out there who may be feeling dismissed: That is not my intention at all. As an expert, I just know what works. So I hope you can accept this information in the spirit in which I offer it (and offer up some super competition to your opponents!).

SPEAKRETS® TOOLKIT

Successful language has three basic components as old as advertising itself:

1. Find a simple, relevant message that your audience will respond to emotionally.

2. Deliver it with passion.

3. Repeat it constantly over a long period of time.

SPEAKRET #14: Cultivate A Tribe Of Die-Hard Fans

-Ruth's Truth-

Instead of creating customers, whom you must chase, create fans, who will chase you.

I miss Steve Jobs. Not only because I love Apple products and credit his vision with their beauty and function. In my professional opinion, Jobs was the greatest CEO presenter of all time. He knew how to put on a show.

In 2010, Steve Jobs received a standing ovation at the event introducing Apple's iPad. People were happy to see him, of course, especially because he was in the midst of a significant and indefinite medical leave. But people also have come to expect the type of presentation that it seems only he could have delivered. It was a phenomenon.

I was so blown away by Jobs's impact as a presenter, there are two places I've written about it in this book (Speakret #15). He embodied the Apple brand. In his black turtleneck and jeans, he was the epitome of Silicon Valley cool. That's what Apple products are, as well, the coolest, most gorgeously designed, slickest devices out there that, under his leadership and vision, became and remain must-haves. (And kudos to Tim Cook, who, since taking over, has come into his own as a presenter, though he is no Steve Jobs.)

Apple presentations are also slick. I know this because I've worked with Apple and it's true at every level of the organization. There is a tremendous effort that goes into creating a presentation that is so beautifully executed and visually striking (slides can be effective, just not the way they're usually done. Speakret #24). And don't be fooled by Jobs's casual delivery – a lot of thought went into that, as well. I always like to say,

"Preparation + Experience = Spontaneity."

Which Comes First: The Product Or The Presentation?

When I have this discussion with CEO clients it seems to boil down to this question: Which came first, the product or the presentation? Most of the time, nuts and bolts executives think the product is the only thing that matters; if it works as promised and the marketing team does its job, it'll sell.

But sometimes, rarely, a Steve Jobs comes along who "thinks different." Not that the product doesn't matter – of course it always does. But that the presentation matters *just as much.* I've been a CEO speech and communications coach a long time and I cannot name another current major corporate executive who places the value and puts the effort into presentation Jobs did. Remember the Google Nexus One Phone, announced and presented to the public with great fanfare in January 2010? No, I didn't think so.

It's all connected.

The Greatest Branding Tools NO ONE Wants To Use!

Jobs didn't have customers as much as he had cultivated a tribe of die-hard fans who had been worried about their leader. We can debate whether it is a good thing for a public company to be so closely identified with its CEO, but what is undeniable is that it worked, making Apple today the world's most valuable company.

Being able to evangelize and speak with passion about your business makes a difference. Especially in these ridiculously competitive times, I characterize these skills as the *greatest marketing and personal branding tools NO ONE wants to use!* So if you do embrace them and polish them up, stop avoiding them and get to work, you'll be miles ahead of your competition.

SPEAKRETS® TOOLKIT

Go to YouTube and search for Steve Jobs' presentations. Watch his presentations and learn.

SPEAKRET #15: Be Excited And Passionate Like Steve Jobs

-Ruth's Truth-

Excitement and passion are contagious. Steve Jobs built an empire with this simple knowledge.

Ok, so I'm obsessed with Steve Jobs. Most people in my line of work are. He was, in my professional opinion, the greatest CEO speaker of all time.

Some years back, at the urging of a friend, I logged onto MacWorld's website to watch a Steve Jobs keynote speech. Though I had certainly heard of his legendary status as a speaker among the Mac faithful, I had never actually seen Jobs present before.

Going in, I expected something truly extraordinary. What I saw was a presentation that was pretty good, but not astounding. The presentation was long – nearly two hours – and much of the time was taken up with a tutorial for the product of the day, the now-iconic iPhone.

Perhaps you're wondering, as I was, how the maestro handled the specifics of a major presentation. Here's a concise recap. Jobs's voice is fairly expressive, but nothing special. His stage presence is quite good; he doesn't stand behind anything and he walks around the stage with a very open posture and broad gestures. He owns it. The slide presentation that he followed was fabulous – very simple and graphically appealing (Speakret #24). Yet, even though the iPhone demo was great fun to watch. I was surprised that I didn't find Jobs especially funny or entertaining.

This led me to think: How in the world did Jobs develop his reputation as a presentation-skills genius within the Apple community? It didn't seem to add up.

Before he concluded, I had my answer: Whatever his limitations when compared to more technically proficient speakers, Steve Jobs has one huge advantage: He connects emotionally with his audience (Speakret #22). He is truly excited about his company, its products, and the people Apple serves. He genuinely likes his audience, and they like him. It's contagious. There is authentic intimacy between speaker and audience. And that is something special.

This leads me to a point worth remembering: If you genuinely like both your subject and your audience, you're halfway home. Speaking or presentation is, after all, about making a connection. If you are willing to show how you truly feel, and if you are shrewd enough to select a subject that genuinely excites you, you can make the same kind of compelling connection to your target audience that Jobs regularly does.

Does it help to have a breakthrough, category-redefining product like the iPhone to show off during your presentation? Sure. But it's not necessary.

SPEAKRETS® TOOLKIT

Follow those three simple principles, and before long, you'll have your own community of true believers:

1. Cultivate a deep belief in and passion for what you're saying and selling.

2. Be willing to actually follow your own advice.

3. Stand behind what you are advocating, even if that means courting someone's disapproval (Speakret #2).

SPEAKRET #16: Join The Video Revolution

-Ruth's Truth-

Learn on-camera presence, a.k.a., VideoCharisma®, or be left behind.

I'm sure that by the time I'm done writing this, the information I impart here will be on the way to being obsolete. I mean it was not too long ago that Cisco folded the Flip Camera tent. That wonderful, revolutionary piece of equipment was a successful start-up only a few short years before that.

Here's another statistic to wrap your head around: 4+ billion YouTube views per day. Per DAY! To give you some context, only a few months ago, I was telling clients 3 billion (and a few months before that, 2). Who knows where it'll be by the time you read this? You just can't ignore these numbers.

A Return To Face-To-Face

Why video and why now?

Humans are wired to connect face-to-face. For the past two decades, however, we've all been relegated to delivering information in writing. I've ranted elsewhere in this book (Speakret #19) about the inadequacy of email, text, and other writing-only forms of communication.

We are in the midst of a video explosion. Google has completely revamped YouTube to take advantage of what it sees as the next revolution – the online video revolution. It now includes the ability to "Hangout" with others using video, live stream to an unlimited, worldwide public audience. Many of its regular users have become YouTube stars. It has channels and shows produced just for this venue. It will even have networks! And YouTube isn't alone. There are startups now being funded that allow us to live stream video directly from our phones!

In case your mind is reeling because you don't know where or how to start, you're scared, and it all seems so complicated, calm down. It's all at your fingertips – no fancy equipment, no need for special lights, wardrobe or makeup, not even a specialized setting or studio. Nope. All you need is a webcam – preferably the one right in your computer (gotta love Macs), a window (for light), something to say and a few minutes to record.

All right, it's a little more complicated than that. There is some startup time involved. But here's the truth: The only way to get better at it is to do it. Like speaking and communicating of any kind, your on-camera technique will only improve if you practice on-camera – and watch the playback. Painful, but necessary.

Now here's a little secret (or Speakret): My celebrity clients all hate watching themselves on video. So they're not all that different from you and me.

Grab, Give, and Go!

People often get hung up on content. But for just about everyone, content is right at your fingertips. As I mentioned, keep your videos short at least until you've cultivated a following that will stick with you for longer ones. You want to give them information they need and can apply right away. Remember WIIFM (What's In It For Me?).

G.O.I. and G.I.D.

Still reluctant to embrace video? G.O.I. What does that stand for? Get. Over. It. Of course, you cannot G.O.I. unless you G.I.D. Get. It. Done.

It will take some time to get it right, but once you do, you'll be making and uploading videos all the time. I now do them at least weekly, having evolved from a beginning where getting even one done every couple of months was a huge chore. And this is important: Do not strive for perfection. People aren't looking for someone who looks perfect and who never stumbles over a single word. They're looking to connect with someone who is more like they are... more like you!

All of my celebrity clients did B-movies and commercials before they got their big break. So don't expect to win the Oscar the first time.

Now, whip out your webcam, phone, or tablet, press "record," and get your show on the air. What a unique and compelling way to draw people to you.

See you on TV!

SPEAKRETS® TOOLKIT

On-Camera Technique:

1. Look into the lens. The lens is where your audience is, where the connection happens.

2. Treat that lens as if it were your best friend or someone else you really like.

3. Make sure your look is consistent with your brand (Speakret #6).

4. If you wear makeup, street makeup is enough. Powder eliminates shine on women and men.

5. Light your face – daylight is best so try to position yourself with a window right in front or, weather permitting, shoot outside.

6. Keep your videos short. Under 2 minutes and preferably under one.

7. Create a YouTube channel (account) and upload your videos to it. Get some feedback from trusted friends.

Easy Content Models:

1. Use content you already have and are expert in that you can repurpose for video.

2. List words/language of your niche and attach a sentence or two of definition to them. Record a video of each one for an eventual video series.

3. Review a book, movie, workshop or something else that connects with your business and gives others good information.

4. Respond to a client query by video instead of phone or email.

5. Include a welcome video for your homepage for immediate bonding.

6. Record videos to accompany your written blog. (This has been hugely successful for me.) For SEO, video combined with text is the most powerful way to get found online.

7. Address FAQs.

8. Provide video testimonials to people who have done right by you.

SPEAKRETS®

SPEAKRET #17: Harness The Enormous Power Of Symbolism

-Ruth's Truth-

Symbols have great meaning. Deploy them with care.

All major presidential speeches are laden with symbolism. In President Obama's State of the Union speeches, the symbolism is especially potent, pervading not only the speech and the surrounding ceremonies, but Congress and beyond.

It's no secret that there has been a huge disconnect between the political parties. Congressional members from opposite sides of the aisle haven't seemed able to get beyond personal attacks. Acrimony has been growing and is at the point where it's difficult, as an observer and citizen to see how anything important can get done. In light of the tremendous problems the country is facing, this development has been very discouraging and disheartening.

In advance of the 2011 State of the Union speech, much had been reported on Congressional Members' efforts to "mix it up," to sit together instead of head to their usual perches on opposite sides of the room. In the days leading up to the speech, it was even referred to as "dating," and, interestingly, fraught with some of the same social complexity and awkwardness teenagers encounter.

I was as doubtful as anyone that this effort would be more than an empty gesture. So I was quite surprised – stunned actually – by the outcome.

Instead of the constant interruptions we've come to expect during the State of the Union, like the loud cheering, jeering, and frequent standing ovations, Members were quieter, more subdued.

While the former behaviors during this particular annual speech make for good theatre, the latter encouraged a more civil and respectful tone than I ever recall seeing.

Just as at a sports event, sitting among the fans of your team encourages a boastful and in-your-face group dynamic. When, however, we are seated among fans of the opposing team, we are somewhat more inhibited and do not feel as free to root for our team so loudly and, perhaps, obnoxiously. Close physical contact forces us to respond to subtle shifts in body language, which is rich in meaning. Call it empathy, call it respect, call it fear of getting beat up... I call it a natural, human instinct to ensure a communication goes smoothly (Speakret #4).

Furthermore, the mere act of sitting next to and getting to know someone with different views makes it all the more difficult to demonize that person later on – or the next day when Members of Congress had to get back to work solving our very serious problems.

The downside is the speech was less entertaining. I actually thought it was boring. But what was sacrificed in drama was gained in a more civil tone.

Of course, the good or inhibited feelings weren't sustained, but it was nice while it lasted.

Symbolic gestures have impact. Good for us all to remember.

SPEAKRETS® TOOLKIT

Think of one or two things you could do in the next month that are weighted enough with symbolism that they will impact relationships positively.

SPEAKRET #18: Become A Media Darling

-Ruth's Truth-

Becoming a media darling is all about reputation management.

Remember when Justin Bieber was a media darling? At that time, not too long ago, I was so impressed I wrote about it because even though he's gone somewhat off the rails since then, the techniques he used worked then and still apply.

I was slow to embrace Justin Bieber. As most people know, Justin grew from a kid with YouTube videos (Speakret #16) to become a teenage pop-singing sensation. With his albums, movies, and media appearances, including on the Grammys, where in 2011 he was the odds-on favorite to win the "Best New Artist" award, Justin's public presence has been ubiquitous.

I hadn't paid him much attention, quite honestly, because I let my prejudices get in the way. I figured what could this kid know? He was only 15! Furthermore, as a professionally trained musician, I wondered how good could he possibly be?

Pretty good, it turned out. In watching him embrace his sudden fame at that time, I was very impressed. Not with his talent so much, though I do think he's got something there. I was floored by his media savvy.

Justin became a media darling because he did the following things very well...

- **Presentation:** He seemed to like and appreciate his fans and showed it. He was always friendly to them, generously spending his time signing autographs and posing for photos.

- **Humility:** Bieber hadn't seemed too taken with himself. He came across as grounded and reality-based. He seemed to recognize his position on the pedestal was tenuous and uncertain. (Oh, boy, was it!)

- **Sense of humor:** Especially about himself, which is the best kind! He didn't seem to take any of the attention he received very seriously.

- **Graciousness:** Justin did not win the "Best New Artist" award in 2011, which he was widely favored to do. In an upset, that award went to someone else. But Bieber handled his loss with grace and poise, expressing happiness for the winner and wishing her well. That was not true for many of his fans, who threw an online hissy fit. They should've taken a page from their idol.

This type of behavior made people like him – especially people who tended to be quick to write him off, like yours truly. It played a big part in enabling him to maintain his superstar status and keep it growing – for a time.

And it exemplified the type of public image that anyone in any business should strive for and master. It's not necessarily about the immense fame, of course (though that might be nice). It's about the manner in which one publicly conducts oneself that draws people in. It is enticing. And if there are doubters, it offers the best chance for another look.

Now, even though his media-savvy has seemed to decline as he has grown up, Justin can look back to see and remember what made him so interesting and such a superstar to begin with. After all, he hasn't lost his talent, just his media mojo. And that he can get back. I wish him well.

SPEAKRETS® TOOLKIT

If you have the opportunity to be covered by the media here are 3 things to bear in mind:

1. Decide on three (3) main messages.

2. Anticipate the most difficult questions you'll get and prepare answers.

3. Practice answering them out loud.

SPEAKRET #19: Face-To-Face Is Still King

-Ruth's Truth-

When it comes to communication, face-to-face is primary. Always has been, always will be.

As someone who works to help business leaders and their corporations communicate better, I know that face-to-face communication is indispensable, and that there is simply no substitute for it. So do they. Even as technology occupies a larger and larger piece of the communication space, making it more difficult to take such a hard line, I take the hard line anyway.

In my speeches that I give (face-to-face), I frequently ask for a show of hands in answer to a series of three questions. They are:

1. "How many of you find that you text or email more than you speak to someone on the phone or

face-to-face?" (At least half the hands always go up.)

2. "How many of you text or email when you should be speaking on the phone or face-to-face?" (More than half of the hands go up.)

3. "How many of you have found that after several rounds of going back and forth by text or email, you pick up the phone or go see the person on the other end and solve the problem in 30 seconds?" (Almost all the hands go up.)

Clearly, speaking can be a more efficient way of coming to agreement or solving a problem than the methods today's technology provides. No matter how instantaneous we think virtual communication is, it is no match for the speed and efficiency of the spoken word. This is not unimportant in a business environment where time has become an increasingly precious commodity.

Yet there is another, even more important benefit than time savings: There is an emotional component to speaking that we work to expunge from writing and let's be clear, text and email are writing. Emotional content fosters connections and we lose the ability to connect on an emotional level when we delegate much, if not most, of our communicating to these written forms.

When we write, the meaning is contained in the words, on the page, in black and white. Sure, we can add italics, underlines, or bolding for emphasis, but that's it. When we speak, however, meaning is largely contained in how, where, and when we say the words. Tone, expression, volume, word emphasis, even accent and dialect, contain information that gives meaning to our words. And that's only the voice (Speakret #8). If we add hand and body movement, facial expression and eye communication, dress and adornment, there is a rich lode of information that just cannot be communicated by words alone (Speakret #26).

Proof of the vital importance of face-to-face communication can be seen the way in which politicians conduct their election campaigns. Take the early presidential contests in the United States: These all-important primaries, at least, are always "retail," face-to-face campaigns, with lots of glad-handing and diner and mom-and-pop shop stops. If they're lucky, they win and graduate to campaigns that use TV in a frantic attempt to recreate the retail experience, e.g., meeting voters in person. It's why TV is so ubiquitous at the highest levels – and why the costs of running a campaign are so high. They want to harness the magic of a face-to-face encounter.

Voters get much more meaningful information about candidates by seeing them, and the more up-close-and-personal, the better. The know-like-trust factor is considerably easier to vet when we have had a chance to meet or at least see a candidate versus only hearing about the candidate or receiving written information about him or her.

This truth is not lost on successful business leaders. While they depend on smart phones and all the other "indispensable" technologies, they also know if they don't actually see their customers, if they don't schmooze their boards, network with their peers, or mingle with their employees, they will be at a significant disadvantage in today's ultra-competitive marketplace.

The Value Of Virtual

At the same time, business leaders know that virtual communication carries significant benefits. For one thing, written information can be looked over and fixed before that fateful moment when we hit the "send" button! This is certainly important when we compose formal documents, where it is expected that organization, grammar and spelling will be correct. The "final version" factor can be important, too, for many informal forms of written communication. Often, we use text and email as a substitute for communicating face-to-face or at least voice-to-voice. Proper spelling and grammar are becoming less important in these types of messages (depending on the recipient and the context), but we can still sit on a missive and think before we hit "send" (Speakret #20).

Another benefit is that we can keep in touch and converse with people who are very far away or with others who may live close by, but with whom we would not ordinarily meet face-to-face. There is no question that this ability to communicate instantly with others all over our planet has been a tremendous boon to business. Does this foster social connections? Well, yes, it does, though it remains a weak substitute for face-to-face, even though it's necessary some times for logistical reasons. Something is always missing.

To me, however, and I think to most people, being connected socially is much more about thinking and feeling than it is about content. A face-to-face meeting or even a phone conversation often has some dead air, moments when two or more people just sit there, without speaking, but thinking and feeling instead, so that the next words are likely to be more thoughtful, and perhaps imbued with some significant emotion.

How important is face-to-face and voice-to-voice communication in an era of Facebook, Twitter, the ever-increasing social media outlets, not to mention text? I think the best answer is that, despite the onslaught of innovative communications technology, and despite the pressure to use alternative methods of contact for everyday communication, face time is still very important indeed... if you want to do really well in business, if you want to make the big money. Yes, there is a time and a place for virtual communication – but when you can, you should find a way to get face-to-face.

SPEAKRETS® TOOLKIT

Go face-to-face when:

1. The outcome is critical.

2. There is a conflict.

3. Things have gotten mucked up in email exchanges.

4. Courting a new client.

5. Pitching a client (existing or new).

SPEAKRET #20: Appreciate Wallflower Power

-Ruth's Truth-

Being shy or introverted is no reason to stay out of the spotlight.

Imagine the scene: A shy person is standing at the entrance to a room full of business people and cannot spot a familiar face. The people are milling about or have arranged themselves into small conversation groups. Attempting to join one of these conversation groups feels rude and intrusive. To add to the dynamic, the din makes effective eavesdropping difficult if not impossible, making it difficult to judge whether elbowing into the conversation even makes sense. The ever-present temptation to simply turn around and walk out the door is rapidly growing stronger because such an internal struggle causes deep feelings of discomfort and saps energy. To top it all off, this shy person will often be thinking, "What can I possibly add to this conversation?" Or worse, "What if they ignore me?"

Now imagine that the person standing at the doorway is not shy. We might describe her as outgoing or extroverted. This person is excited and energized by the prospect of meeting new people and making new contacts, of listening to what others are saying and speaking herself. This individual looks at this scenario as a game, a challenge that will help to sharpen skills and make progress toward becoming a better and more recognizable player. It is viewed as a challenge that is begging to be overcome. Thoughts of this non-shy person may include, "I can really influence this conversation," or "Let's see what value I can add." Being ignored never even enters the picture. This person relishes the give and take that this type of activity offers. It is fun being in the spotlight, winning the game.

Interestingly, both of these approaches require a level of self-consciousness with the shy person thinking, "I have nothing to add," and the non-shy person thinking just the opposite. In both cases, the individual is internally focused. It is in the shy case, however, that the focus is tinged with negativity. It is this tendency to ascribe negative meaning that shy people must work to change.

As a shy – and introverted – person myself, I've come to discover over the years that shyness takes many forms and occurs on many levels. Whatever form it takes, it is something that can be managed and integrated into professional life.

When Shyness is Good

Although most people would not choose to be shy, there are some benefits to shyness. Shy people tend to be better listeners and have more empathy with others than the non-shy. As children, they tend to be better students and are less likely to engage in disruptive behavior. When responding to a survey on shyness that I sent to a thousand people, a significant number of respondents who identified themselves as shy or shy-leaning said they felt they were better team players because they were not inclined to want a starring role. They felt they were more sensitive to other people's moods and could read nonverbal cues more effectively making them the type of workers that other employees felt comfortable opening up to. They were not as likely to display extreme emotions.

In fact, shy people are some of the most productive workers. Shy employees are focused and less likely to succumb to the many distractions inherent in the workplace. They are more likely to get along with their bosses and co-workers. The increased level of social sensitivity – and inactivity – that is exhibited by shy people, benefits everyone around them.

When Shyness is a Problem

While employers and co-workers benefit, though, the shy do suffer from the detrimental effects of their behavior. Like it or not, the workplace these days compels employees to acquire and master communication skills that are anathema to most shy people. The ability to fully participate and speak in meetings, attend and exploit business/social events, sell the company products, services and ideas or deliver a stand-up presentation to a group is commonly expected. In addition, promotions, bonuses, raises, awards and other types of recognition, not to mention getting hired in the first place all depend on the types of self-promotional skills the shy employee generally recoils from.

A particularly entrenched and well-documented problem for the shy is a reluctance to ask for help. Asking for help indicates that you don't know something or are having difficulty. It exposes weaknesses and deficits, which, in turn increase the potential for embarrassment and humiliation, a very frightening prospect for the shy. If we think about it, this reluctance to ask for help can be very damaging. For example, it is well known that finding a good mentor is an excellent way to learn about a job or business. But the mere thought of having a relationship that has been formalized into helper and "helpee" pushes all the shy buttons.

While no one likes to be embarrassed or humiliated, the non-shy are able to put themselves out there time and again regardless of the risk of rejection. Shy people, on the other hand, build fortresses to protect themselves from such risks. Of course, such barriers do not discriminate; they keep out the good as well as the bad. The final result of all these machinations is that shy people are caught in a seemingly intractable double bind because as we all know, unless you put yourself out there, there is no way to know if what you are doing is valued.

An Introvert In An Extroverted World

We live in a culture that exalts celebrity and exhibitionism. With the plethora of reality shows, we have all been made into voyeurs and peeping toms. But these developments have made the shy feel even more inadequate than they already do and become even more withdrawn. It is the shy person's worst nightmare.

Yet it is just this type of isolating behavior that shy people must change to succeed. Study after study has shown that up to 50% of the population identifies as shy. This corresponds to my own, relatively small survey. When I began to speak to people about shyness, I found that the answers were all over the map. Some people were shy about striking up a conversation with strangers. Others were shy in their personal lives but not at work. Most people were shy about some things, but not others. Then there were people who said they used to be shy, but are not shy anymore. And still others who found they suddenly became shy after some incident occurred in their lives.

Wherever it may come from, if you are shy, know that you far from alone. There are millions upon millions of shy people out there. You are interacting and talking with other shy people every, single day. You just may not know it.

What I have discovered, both as a shy person myself and from speaking with many others is that there are excellent strategies that we shy people can use and by doing so, help us effectively manage our shyness and achieve the success we crave and deserve.

SPEAKRETS® TOOLKIT

The following strategies are guaranteed to help you become the boss of your shyness:

- *Enlist a mentor or hire a coach.*

- *Practice your introductory pitch and have it ready to go.*

- *Go to networking events and force yourself to practice entering conversations (and delivering your introductory pitch).*

- *Get yourself booked as a speaker (See Section 3, PUBLIC SPEAKRETS® for help).*

- *Know you are NOT alone.*

PART THREE: PUBLIC SPEAKRETS®

Study, practice, and master these principles ... so you can become publicly identified as a powerful communicator and presenter.

SPEAKRETS®

SPEAKRET #21: Master The Platform

-Ruth's Truth-

Polished, confident presentation skills are unsurpassed methods of increasing your personal and professional impact.

Think about the last time you attended a conference and saw an outstanding speaker. After the presentation, you wanted to meet that speaker. You even stood in line, patiently waiting for your turn. Why? You wanted to be in that speaker's professional network, included in their sphere of influence. During the rest of the conference, you noticed people seeking out the speaker and talking about the presentation. Suddenly, it seemed, the speaker was a star.

If you've ever wished for this type of "overnight success," I've got great news... your wish can come true!

Presentation Story One

I attend a lot of events and see a lot of speakers. Some are great, others not so much. A segment of one event I attended determined the title of this Speakret. The segment featured opportunities for entrepreneurs to stand up and deliver their business pitch to a panel of experts and receive feedback. Five experienced entrepreneurs volunteered to take turns pitching.

The first three received some tough criticism. Their presentations came across as weak and timid. Their body language was hesitant and shy. They were inarticulate when describing their work. One even asked the panel if she should get some presentation coaching. (I yelled out, "Yes!" Couldn't help myself.) The panel's common critique for all three was that after listening to them, they still didn't know what they did or how they made money.

The final two then had their turns in the hot seat. These entrepreneurs presented themselves well. They came across as sure and certain, looking and sounding confident. They made direct eye contact and didn't seem cowed or intimidated by the panel, who were subsequently complimentary.

Here's what got my attention: These two entrepreneurs said virtually the same thing as the first three. Their words were disjointed and not particularly well-organized. I did not learn any more about what these two did or how they made money. But because they said it in a more poised and polished way, the panel felt they had done a good job. Their nonverbal behaviors made them more believable.

Presentation Story Two

I was recently charged with listing a house for sale on behalf of an elderly relative. I interviewed two realtors. Realtor One had a relationship with the family. Realtor Two was a stranger who'd been highly recommended. When Realtor One came in, her presentation was disorganized and disjointed. I found it difficult to understand why she priced the house as she did. The comparables were missing the selling prices and were not in order.

Realtor Two was polished. She and her associate had it all together. In addition, she'd been in touch with me prior to our meeting to notify me of a mistake in the tax rolls pertaining to the house, something that would have to be fixed.

Both these professionals were experienced and could have done an equally good job. It was a tough choice because of the existing relationship and subsequent pressure to favor Realtor One. Ultimately, the presentation was the deciding factor. Realtor Two cared, wanted the business. It demonstrated to me a level of organization that is key in the business with all its paperwork and legalities. She got the listing.

When Realtor One called to find out why she'd lost out, I tried to fluff it off. But she wanted to know, so I told her the presentation was the issue. To her credit, she agreed and told me she'd been embarrassed. She also told me the realtor I chose was a top expert, someone she truly liked and had worked with for many years and was glad that if it couldn't be her, I chose the other. That was generous of her. See what I mean about it having been a tough choice?

Style v. Substance? Think French Food

To those who question whether good presentation is merely style over substance, I refer them to French Food. The French are known throughout the world for their delicious, well-prepared food. They are also known for the way they present it. When a plate of fine French food is set in front of you, it looks delicious. Your mouth waters and you can't wait to take a bite. That doesn't mean the food will be delicious, but presentation makes you receptive and more likely to believe it is.

Here is the corollary: While the ability to present and speak in public with confidence and poise can never take the place of substance, it can push substantive deficiencies into the background and present opportunities less polished communicators (with great substance) will not receive.

The lesson is that a good presentation can easily mean the difference between winning and losing. Beyond that, it can open doors and provide opportunities for a second look. Confidence in oneself instills confidence in others.

SPEAKRETS® TOOLKIT

Improving your presentation skills requires training...

- Toastmasters, a world-wide speaking club, dedicated to helping speakers improve

- National Speakers Association, based in the United States, has chapters in almost every state

- Private coaches

and experience...

- Local business groups

- Conferences and conventions

- Client luncheons or events

SPEAKRET #22: Get Emotional

-Ruth's Truth-

Strategically deploy emotions to connect and be relatable.

Putting feeling into what you're saying by using powerful words, gestures, and facial expressions as a conduit for your emotions is essential if you wish to connect with your audience and stakeholders. Of course, many people are reluctant to show their feelings. Emotional displays are often considered to be unprofessional. We're not talking here about bursting into tears, yelling and screaming, or behaving in any other way that may be considered to be extreme. To be successful as speakers, however, we must be willing to express ourselves and take some risks in doing so.

We've all seen speakers who, reluctant to show how they feel, deliver their material in a monotone voice with stiff physical presence (or no presence at all). These speakers often have good information; the material may be well researched and much needed by their audiences. Yet they are afraid to become intimate with their listeners. In many cases, they fail to communicate their messages in any meaningful way, resulting in a waste of time for all concerned.

Some of the fears that give rise to this problem are the result of people's early training. Their parents may have told them that public displays of emotion were unseemly or poor manners. Others fear coming off as "too slick." Many a client of mine has expressed concerns about coming off as too "sales-y" or too theatrical. One client, a senior executive at a large, prestigious, private bank, was planning to take some wealthy, A-list, bold-face-named clients on a retreat to a luxury resort where clients would attend workshops on financial planning and investing led by these bankers. The bankers were very worried that they might be seen as "selling too much." My response was that the wealthy clients who had accepted the bank's invitation were busy professionals who did not need a free vacation. The reason they were there was to hear about new services and products that would help them protect and grow their enormous wealth. They wanted to be "sold." Once my client realized this, he and his team felt much freer to display passion about their business, and the retreat was a big success.

Communicate Your Passion

Leaders are very focused on their expertise. This makes perfect sense. The problem arises when they only tell how expert they are and even why their point of view is the right one. However, if you believe what you are speaking about, it shouldn't be too difficult to inject some feeling into the vocal and physical display. If you don't believe what you are speaking about, don't panic! This situation is more common than you may realize. In such a situation, you have a number of options: You can find another topic, find another job (I know, I know), or make a commitment to try to find things about your pitch that you do believe in, and focus on them.

The next step is to put yourself in your listener's shoes. This is something effective speakers must do all the time; it is an incredibly difficult task. It's tough to be objective. But, if you are the type of person who practices what you preach, you should be able to do an honest assessment, and view your topic from your listener's perspective.

The third step may be the most important of all: Get uncomfortable. This is where risk is involved and audience disapproval is one of the scariest risks that most people can think of. No one likes to be disapproved of, but my experience is that if you take the risk of showing your true feelings to your audience, they will respond positively (Speakret #2).

Now, what are some of the things you can do to begin putting more feeling into what you're saying? Well, to begin with, your voice is a huge component (Speakret #8). There are so many things we can do with our voices; we can raise or lower the volume, use a wide range of pitch and expression, and speed up or slow down our rate of speech.

Next, your body language must support what you are saying (Speakret #26). Posture, hands, voice, facial expression, eye contact all serve to confirm your position and role.

SPEAKRETS® TOOLKIT

There are three critical questions you should ask yourself when trying to inject emotional content into what you are saying:

1. Do you believe what you are speaking about?

2. Would you take your own advice?

3. Are you willing to be uncomfortable?

SPEAKRET #23: Find The Best Stories

-Ruth's Truth-

Stories make otherwise dry and boring information come alive.

We have all endured presentations where the information being delivered was dry, boring, and tedious. We sit there and daydream, disengaging from the speaker, and wishing for the show to end... or for the courage to get up and leave before the end. Our original reason for going was to get information that would help us to do our job better or grow our business. If we're lucky during these types of presentations, we pick up a few pointers and do our best to incorporate them... while wondering why sitting through the presentation to get that information had to be such a chore.

It doesn't have to be that way. The most effective, persuasive communicators and presenters tell stories and use sayings, quotes, and humor during their presentations. They know that weaving this material into their speaking makes things entertaining for their audiences, illustrates points, and proves that the presenter is someone very much like them, with similar experiences and perspectives.

Where Are The Stories?

This is a big challenge for most of my clients, who do not consider themselves natural storytellers. Once we sit together during the early part of our engagement, the stories begin to flow. Whether you work with someone like me to help you tease out your many wonderful stories or not, you can find story material you can use just about everywhere. In fact, most of us are good enough storytellers already; we just haven't figured out how to connect them to our presentations and speeches.

The first place to look is your own life. Chances are excellent that if you sit down and brainstorm your own personal stories – the times you learned something significant – you will come up with several very good, usable anecdotes that can be included in your presentations. Personal stories by their nature are genuine, and audiences pick up on that. Audiences long for intimacy with speakers and these types of anecdotes are a terrific way to create it. The stories can be business or personal, but either way, should relate to the point being made. You don't have to concoct some long saga; often, a simple but telling insight from your own experience will be just as effective. For example, as an opening to a presentation on business strategy to a company that had gotten well behind the curve in its Internet strategy, one speaker I worked with compared the situation with "not having a phone in the house." This was a perfect and dramatic verbal illustration of just how serious the situation was at this company. It grabbed the audience and they listened raptly for the rest of the presentation.

Another speaker I know of told a story about how difficult it had been for him to delegate work to employees; he bravely related to the audience his own fears about giving up control. The moral to the story was that, once he did learn to delegate, his profits soared. After telling that story – one utterly unique to his own experience – he was then able to communicate to his audience, step-by-step, just how he did it. As you can imagine, they were completely engaged by this point – much more so than they would have been had he simply started sharing "how to" points without offering his own emotionally rich personal experiences.

Still someone else, in a presentation on growing a business, told the story of facing tough times in what was then her $1 million dollar business. She explained how going to a business development workshop and hearing the words "straight commission" was a transformational moment for her. Her business now grosses $30 million.

There are plenty of quotes, quips and stories available in books and online. One of the best is Bartleby.com This is a collection aggregated from several sources that encompasses a treasure trove of quotes from famous speakers dating back to the ancient Romans and Greeks. It is cross-indexed by both quote and speaker, so if you don't remember a quote exactly, but have some of the words or know the theme, you can still find the right story. It's indispensable.

Even though Bartleby.com is my favorite, there are many other such sites available covering a multitude of quotations that can be found under every possible search rule or cross-reference.   Try Quotations.com, Quotes.com or if, for example, you're looking for a quote by Mark Twain, just search for "Mark Twain Quotes" and numerous options will show up.

Newspapers and magazines are excellent resources that will often contain relevant articles. Bookmark the ones you see online and categorize them. Or, open a file on your computer, make regular "story deposits," and watch your treasury grow.

Personal Stories Are The Best Stories

Even with all the material available to the public, the best resource for impactful storytelling is you. Personal stories are best. Many speakers create a unique, compelling story to let audiences get closer to them (sometimes referred to as a "signature story"). These stories are often about overcoming adversity or how they were once poor, but are now rich. Generally, they are designed to draw audiences closer, let them know they are not alone. These types of stories connect speaker and audience and motivate them to believe they can do it, too – whatever "it" is.

I try to not get too serious with my stories, even when making a serious point. I look for humor, particularly self-directed humor and deploy it. It can be very effective without making people squirm. And when I say "humor," I don't mean jokes like the comedians use. There are funny and ironic things that happen to all of us almost daily and if we're disciplined and capture them, we can end up with quite a collection.

Mold Your Story To Suit The Occasion

You should also keep in mind that a good story can usually be molded to fit the occasion. And you don't have to be completely accurate. For example, if a relevant story or quip happened last year, but fits within the current presentation and would have more impact if it happened yesterday, then skip the time reference and let the audience assume it happened yesterday. The idea is to get the most impact with material you've got. I have stories I've used for years that are just as relevant today as when I first told them. So do other professional speakers.

Telling stories and using quotes and quips to spice up your presentation are wonderful ways to plug into your audience and have them plug right back into you. There is magic in the art of storytelling. Practice that art, and you'll have the ability to have the audience eating out of your hand whenever you want.

SPEAKRETS® TOOLKIT

Keep a "Content Journal." This is simply a file or place that you can jot down story ideas the minute they pop into your head. Here are just a few general resources for stories...

1. Personal stories

2. Business stories

3. Favorite quotes

4. Current events

5. Cool statistics

6. Movies, TV and pop culture

7. Books

8. Travel experiences

SPEAKRET #24: Stop Using Slides

-Ruth's Truth-

Try to rid yourself of slides. If you must use them, however, use very few, make them bold, graphic, and easy to read.

I'm on a mission to expunge slides from all my clients' presentations. PowerPoint is the main culprit. But Keynote, too... sorry Apple.

(Note: There is a very cool program called Prezi that offers an alternative to the current ubiquitous PowerPoint or Keynote decks. It's online at prezi.com. Check it out.)

For a while, I thought things were actually getting better on this front. People seemed to be using fewer slides, though they were as poorly designed as ever. Alas, there seems to have been a relapse. Maybe it's because

Microsoft and now Apple come out with new bells and whistles every couple of years or so, and the temptation to use them is just too great to resist.

Option one, of course, is to just say "No" to slides. I know it's hard to break this addiction and your workplace may expect slides, so if you can't say no, follow the ten steps in this chapter's Speakrets® Toolkit.

Of course, I realize that, with an addiction as powerful as this one, expecting people to do away with slide decks entirely is probably unrealistic. There is much more to this topic - but these techniques should at least start you on the road to recovery.

SPEAKRETS® TOOLKIT

In lieu of going cold turkey (which really is the first and best option) here are a few techniques that will improve any presentation ... and also support the long-term weaning process.

1. **Limit the number of slides.** These days, it is not unusual for a 30-minute presentation to contain 30-40 slides. THIS IS WAY TOO MUCH! For a 30-minute presentation, choose the 5-10 most important slides. (Hint: 5 is far better — and braver — than 10.)

2. **Limit the information on each slide.** There should be no more than 4-5 bulleted or chart items on a slide. They should function as triggers or cues for elaboration vs. complete sentences or paragraphs.

3. **Make sure the slide is readable.** Body copy should be at least 18 points. 20 points or larger is better. Headlines show up well at a minimum of 36 points. Use upper and lower case and a consistent, simple font.

4. **Use message headings.** Instead of a slide with a headline that says "Performance," which in reality tells the audience nothing about performance, consider a more complete thought, such as "Company X significantly outperformed the S&P through day/month/year.

5. **Use animation and other bells and whistles sparingly.** Most special effects are useless. There are, however, at least two winning effect: the slide transition (from slide-to-slide). The first is "cover down" and the second is "cube left." These effects create a smooth, professional transition from slide to slide and far outperform the default transition.

6. **Automate effects as much as possible.** There may be an item or two on an occasional slide that you would like to control by mouse click, but if you're clicking for each item to appear, trust me, that's too much work for you and too much "noise" for the audience.

7. **Simpler is better.** Although you could design a 3-D pie chart to illustrate some information, you

might be surprised to see that a 2-D chart is actually more effective. This is a principle to apply to all your slides. Save the fancy footwork for your speaking.

8. **Make liberal use of the "B" key.** Most people don't know this, but if you press the letter B on your keyboard during a PowerPoint presentation, the screen will go dark. This puts the focus back on you. When you're ready to move on, press B again and you'll find yourself right where you left off.

9. **Do not use a laser pointer.** I don't know whose brilliant idea this little piece of technology was, but not only it is distracting and ineffective, it magnifies every movement or tremor of your hand. Can you say "Stage Fright?"

10. **Practice with your slides.** Never wait until the presentation to see what it looks like on screen. The projector you use may display colors quite differently than your laptop. This can make for some unpleasant surprises. Address these ahead

of time, before an audience is present. (Speakret #5.)

SPEAKRET #25: Channel The Power Of Stage Fright

-Ruth's Truth-

Stage Fright goes with the territory. It can help you be amazing so don't fight it – use it.

At this point, I probably don't have to remind you that landing an assignment to deliver a speech or presentation can shake the confidence of even the most experienced professional. Does it have to be so threatening? Well, sort of - and here's why.

There are some inherent aspects of presenting that are unavoidable. The first is that in general, it is an individual activity. You and you alone will be standing and speaking before a group. All eyes will be on you. The result of this increased scrutiny is that any error has the potential to be more glaring than in other types of communicating. The stakes (for you) are higher and success or failure more meaningful. You will probably feel intimidated and worry about how you will perform. We call this state of anxiety Stage Fright.

Stage Fright Makes You Better – Really!

Anyone who has ever been on a stage is familiar with the feeling. Your heart races, perspiration increases, hands tremble, mouth goes dry. Even the most skilled and prepared actors and speakers feel it. It's a natural reaction to a perceived threat and is also known as fight or flight, the survival mechanism that makes us better able to fight off or run away from danger. The powerful chemicals that are instantly released make us stronger, faster and more agile. What is less well known, though, is that fight or flight also makes us quicker witted, better able to think on our feet and make split-second decisions. In a way, it makes us smarter.

The feeling, however, is so unpleasant for most people that they push back against it, ignore it or even chide themselves for having it, which just make it worse. Skilled speakers know a secret (or Speakret) about Stage Fright: It helps make them more animated, more exciting to watch and better at delivering their presentation. So instead of worrying about it, they embrace it.

There is a caveat: Stage Fright works its magic best when you are prepared. Just as someone who is physically fit and experienced would be better able to fight off or flee from danger, so would a presenter who was well-prepared and/or who had experience be much better able to make Stage Fright work positively. The ability to think more quickly on your feet allows you to deal seamlessly with the inevitable things that go wrong in every presentation instead of allowing them to derail you.

About Those Inevitable Mistakes...

We are human. Therefore mistakes are unavoidable. This is not to say we can't keep them to a minimum. And, once again, being well rehearsed helps manage the errors and stumbles (Speakret #5). Even the most experienced and accomplished speakers make mistakes despite ample practice. Their secret (or Speakret) is that they know how to recover. For example:

- If the mistake is small enough so that you can be reasonably sure no one has noticed, do not get flustered or call attention to it in any way. Even if it is slightly noticeable to someone, it is extremely unlikely that they will hold it against you.

- If the mistake is glaring, calmly take care of it and try to use humor to call attention away from the mistake and toward your humanity.

By the way, you do not have to apologize, so don't!

You will be fondly remembered for your grace under pressure. In the unlikely event you find yourself losing control, it is acceptable to take a few seconds to collect yourself. This is a good time to have a sip of water, which you should always have nearby.

Disparity And Exaggeration

Many of us have had the experience of being in a stressful situation and feeling as if time has slowed to almost a standstill while we are speaking publicly. In reality, of course, time is chugging right along at its usual pace. When presenting, a situation in which stress is inherent, any error, no matter how small, seems glaring to the speaker. In many cases, the mistake or pause is not even noticed by the audience. Still it is difficult to move on as if nothing has happened. So, we tend to become more stressed and flustered and thus we call attention to ourselves unnecessarily. This feeling of the speaker's perception being contradicted by the audience's perception is known as disparity.

Disparity is almost universal and goes with the territory, much in the same way that stage fright does. There is really no way to make a speaker feel it differently. But you can choose to see it differently, and I mean this literally. Videotaping your performances is proof-positive that a disparity of perception exists and this knowledge alone is usually enough to quiet those extra nerves.

Exaggeration is related to disparity. In an exercise I conduct during some training seminars and workshops, participants are asked to exaggerate a gesture – to make it very big – as big as possible. Afterward, we ask the other participants for feedback and we also watch the video. We almost always notice that the gesture was not nearly as big as it felt to the participant. We do this exercise because gestures and similar forms of nonverbal communication may feel big and over-done. Often, however, they are not. In fact, much of the time the opposite is true – the gestures are much too small and ineffective.

I believe exaggeration should always be on the mind of the speaker, because although there is such a thing as over-exaggeration, I very rarely see it done in a presentation or speech.

Remember that there is a disparity between your perception and your listeners' perceptions. Exaggeration helps to counteract disparity and should be done as a matter of course, especially before larger audiences.

Bottom line: Stage fright is your friend. Hard to believe, but true. Its presence simply indicates that you care about your performance. That can't be bad.

SPEAKRETS® TOOLKIT

Here are some rejoinders when you make the mistakes that won't just go away...

1. Let me try that again...

2. Whoops, that was a big one. Here's what I meant to say...

3. I'm going to back up and see if I can spit it out...

4. Having a little trouble with my mouth today...

5. Having a bit of a brain freeze...

SPEAKRET #26: Crack The Nonverbal Codes

-Ruth's Truth-

Nonverbal communication gives meaning to your words and makes you believable.

In my professional opinion, 6 years into his presidency, Barack Obama's biggest liability continues to be his inability to show instead of tell.

What do I mean by this? The President's strong inclination to remain above the fray, to avoid showing his feelings, has significantly impacted his ability to lead. He has the idea that it's what you say that should matter, not how you say it. He's very wrong. Voters look to their leaders to connect the dots on their behalf, wanting answers to the following:

1. Can you feel what I do? Do you know what my life is like?

2. Can you change my life for the better?

3. Can you articulate a unifying vision I can get behind?

4. Do you have convictions and believe passionately in them?

Whether you're a CEO, a small business owner or the President of the United States, the people you lead and serve look to you to give their concerns voice and if you fail to do that, they will cast you aside and look for someone who will. And the way that is done is by showing your feelings, not telling about them.

The ability to show, not just tell when communicating is the single, most important skill for a leader. Allowing your feelings to show won't make you seem "sales-y" or theatrical – but real, enabling you to connect with your listeners – and keep them coming back to you for more.

And the only way to "show, not tell" is through the way you look, move, and sound.

So you've gotten an assignment to deliver that presentation and you're well into the preparation process. You already understand that preparation is key (Speakret #5) and that a certain energizing amount of stage fright goes with the territory (Speakret #25).

This chapter is about nonverbal communication: How you say what you say. Basically, nonverbal communication gives your words meaning. It makes you believable. We've all watched presenters who stand up there and do a data dump, look uncomfortable, and deliver their remarks without any passion or conviction. Besides being incredibly boring and tedious, this type of behavior conveys they'd rather be somewhere else and even, possibly, that they can't do their job!

Info-tain

Like a politician, the job of a business speaker is to inform, engage and entertain, and not necessarily in that order. My good friend and colleague, Jennifer Abernethy likes to call it, "info-tain." Clients are always worried about that last directive, that if they try too hard to be entertaining, they'll come off as too slick or phony. I have never seen this happen. I have, however, seen audiences in various states of, shall we say, "relaxation." Audience members playing with their hair, reading, thumbing their smartphones or, worst of all, nodding off. So how do you keep people awake and interested? One major way is via careful and deliberate use of nonverbal communication.

Following is a list of the primary nonverbal codes and how to use them so your message has the very best chance of being heard.

- **Voice**. I've already gone into great detail in Speakret #8, so I won't repeat myself here. I will say, though, that voice is the most loaded of the codes and has the advantage of having an impact whether people can see you or not.

- **Body and Movement.** When walking to the platform, stride purposefully. Your goal should be to command the stage, to own it. Posture should be erect, but not military. Leaning slightly toward your audience is engaging. Once on stage, move with purpose and try not to "dance." It's fine to step toward and away from the audience or to move to one or the other side of the screen (if you're using visuals), but any movement should have a meaning. And definitely avoid pacing from side to side.

- **Eyes.** It's important to build rapport with your audience by looking at them. If it's a fairly small group (20 or fewer), you should try for contact with each person. In a large group, take in small groups. Don't expect them to look back at you. If they look away, move on and come back to them later. During a presentation to a very large group, choose a person in the audience. The people surrounding that person will think you are looking at them. So you will be able to take many people in at one time. Avoid scanning—going back and forth as if watching a tennis match (I call this "Wimbledon"). If you're seated at a conference table, don't forget to look at the people to your immediate left and right.

- **Facial Animation.** There is a fantastic range of movement in the facial muscles that can communicate a tremendous amount of information. Your face should reflect your feelings. If you have an interesting piece of information, it could be reflected in a raised brow. Smiling shows positive feelings and, of course, frowns convey negative ones. I include head movement (tilt, turning away) in this category.

- **Dress and Adornment (Speakret #6).** This refers to everything you weren't born wearing, all the choices we make in clothing, accessories, hairstyle and makeup. The choices range widely. A good rule, however, is to see what the highly regarded people in your workplace or the industry wear during their presentations and emulate them. It also doesn't hurt to ask someone in authority.

Gestures are in a category all by itself, so you'll have to read Speakret #27.

Compensate for Nonverbal Weaknesses With Your Nonverbal Strengths

There is a play I saw recently by Pulitzer winner, Paula Vogel, entitled, "The Long Christmas Ride Home" in which puppets played some of the roles. They were not in the "Sesame Street" or "Avenue Q" mold with cartoonish faces and bodies, and silly character voices. These puppets were human looking. Their faces were painted on, so they couldn't emote. But their bodies were not fixed and their movements, which were manipulated by the enormously skilled actors/ puppeteers, were incredibly expressive. This manipulation made these puppets seem alive. They were at one point funny, and then they would break your heart.

This struck me because I always talk about the nonverbal aspects of speech and that when we're speaking and communicating, we need it all, including facial expression. But we're not all strong in every area. Some people make more effective gestures, others have fabulous, expressive voices, and so on.

My point is that you should play to your strengths and keep working on your weaknesses. I've named it the principle of "communication compensation." If you play up your strong skills, your weaker skills will fade into the background.

But not forever.

This isn't advice to leave your weaker skills as they are – no, no. Rather it's to tell you that the principle allows you to keep working on them so they become as strong as your compensating skills. It gives you some breathing room. So, unlike the puppets in the play, whose faces will never change, you have a chance to do just that.

At the same time, while you're working on it, know that not everything has to be perfect. You won't ever be as strong in some areas as in others. But it won't matter.

Altogether, these nonverbal codes will make you a much more interesting speaker, more capable of grabbing your audience and holding them until you, not they, are done.

SPEAKRETS® TOOLKIT
What's Your NQ - Your Nonverbal Quotient?

Nonverbal Code	Weak or Strong?	How to Improve?
Posture		
Stance		
Facial Expression		
Voice (tone, expression, diction, rate, pace, volume, accent, dialect)		
Eye contact/ communication		
Dress & Adornment		
Hand gestures (Speakret #27)		

SPEAKRETS®

SPEAKRET #27: Let Your Hands Do Some Talking

-Ruth's Truth-

Gestures enrich our words and help us think.

Gestures comprise a Speakret of their very own.

Whenever I'm teaching a presentation skills workshop or working with a high-level client on an important speech, the topic of hand gestures inevitably comes up. Clients aren't quite sure what to do with their hands, so they naturally look for a convenient parking spot: Pockets, arms folded, and clasped behind the back are favorites.

When engaged in informal conversation, however, these same people move their hands and arms naturally and in tune with what they are saying. No coaching required. When I point this out (or play back some video of them talking to me, so they can see what they do when they think they're not being observed), my clients are amused, abashed, and intrigued. They are still bewildered, though, because, even after seeing the video, they cannot figure out how to get their hands to accompany them in a natural way when they make the leap from "private" communication to "public."

Recent research and discoveries about gestures are enlightening. A particularly fascinating piece of information is this: If there is a culture that communicates without gestures, it hasn't been discovered yet! In addition, blind people gesture and so do deaf people, in addition to signing!

Furthermore, research has shown that gestures aid learning. While teaching a group of young learners how to solve a math problem, Susan Wagner Cook of the University of Iowa used specific gestures to emphasize each step in a problem as she taught it. She then asked the students to orally repeat the words and mimic her gestures. A second group of students was taught the same problem minus the gestures and with a third group, more abstract gestures were used - the kind most of us make when speaking. Three weeks later, all the students were tested. The two groups that had learned to solve the problems with both speech and gestures (either specific or abstract) were three times more likely to solve the equation correctly than those who had learned with spoken words alone.

It is well known in the professional development community that adults need visual stimuli even more than young learners. For example, when we give our limited and precious time to attend presentations, most of us want to "take something away" from the talk. Unfortunately, too many times the speaker does not move, grabs onto the podium as though shipwrecked, or stands before us with hands parked permanently in one of the positions I described earlier. When this happens, teaching and learning are hindered and adult learners "take away" less than we deserve to.

Hand Gestures Help Us Think

 Okay, one more piece of research that I absolutely love and then I'll leave you alone:

In addition to giving us teaching and learning benefits, our hands actually help us think! Consider all the times when you are speaking and find yourself struggling to find the right word or phrase. Now try to recall what your hands are doing at these moments. In all likelihood, they're moving in some interesting ways, as if by waving them around, you will pluck from deep in your brain just the word or phrase you are looking for.

In fact, neuroscientists, linguists and psychologists who study speech have found that when someone is doing mental math problems, the part of the brain associated with gestures increases in activity. And when the person gestures, the part of the brain responsible for speech is activated. Researchers therefore believe there is a strong connection between gesturing and problem solving. They theorize that gestures "lighten the cognitive load."

In Constant Motion

What all this means is that during a presentation, your hands and arms should be in almost constant motion. To get some insight, start paying very close attention to how your hands and others' hands move during informal, everyday communicating. That's what should be happening on the platform. Avoid placing your hands in your pockets, folding your arms, or putting your hands behind your back. Down at your sides is the place they should start. By the way, for some reason, this position feels terrible, but looks good.

Be careful not to use a single gesture too repetitively. If you're having difficulty with this, it's a fine idea to choreograph a couple of moves ahead of time. Often, that's enough to get you going.

Be Expansive

Another technique is to be expansive. As with the other nonverbal codes, there is a set of gestures you use for interpersonal speaking and another set for public speaking. Let your arms and hands move away from your body. Remember, you have the entire stage to fill and though you cannot literally do so, you can create a very substantial illusion that will keep all eyes on you. The size and scope of your gestures should reflect the size and scope of the room.

Pretend You're A Super-Hero

One more benefit of hand gestures is the way they help to channel nervous energy every speaker feels (Speakret #25). When I'm on stage, to calm my inevitable jitters, I find it very helpful to envision myself as a superhero who can shoot electricity from my fingertips. (Now you know one of my silly secrets.)

With gesturing such an important part of communication, perhaps we should rethink the rush toward tele-seminars, webinars and other online and remote, non-visual forms of teaching and learning. While I do believe there is a need for all these technologies, they may require modification and adaptation to keep people engaged, such as video (Speakret #16). And they will never offer the kind depth and connection that comes with seeing a person in action.

SPEAKRETS® TOOLKIT

Start being intentional about observing how you – and others – use hand gestures in conversations and other types of speaking. See what works and what doesn't.

SPEAKRETS®

SPEAKRET #28: Keep It Short, Keep Their Attention

-Ruth's Truth-

No one ever objects to a short presentation.

Cleaning out my basement was one of the hardest chores I've ever had to do. We'd accumulated a lot of stuff over 20 years of living in our home and, for some reason, I often resisted getting rid of certain items. I would think I would use them again. Someday. Can you feel me?

One of the tasks people hate most is throwing away well-loved items, and that definitely applies to material they've developed for communication and presentations. It's difficult to stay objective when it comes to something you've created and want to share. After all your hard work, you may find yourself clinging to anything and everything you've gathered.

If you ever find yourself in such a position, just think about cleaning out your attic or getting ready for a tag sale – and remember the decision to rid yourself of all that clutter. Well, that's the idea behind editing and keeping things short. The bad news is that it can be just as painful. We get very attached to the things we create, whether or not they detract from our message.

Keep in mind that editing requires some initial distance. Provided you have some time, I suggest that after you finish composing your presentation, you do not look at it for a day or two. This gives you the space necessary to relax and come back to it with a fresh eye. You know how we can notice typos and other mistakes in a document after giving things a rest for a little while? This process is similar.

Take a break. When you do go back to the presentation, you will probably see things you no longer like or notice certain areas that do not flow very well. There may also be weak transitions or even key points that you decide are extraneous. Throw them out and be absolutely "Ruth-less" about it! I promise you will never miss them and neither will your audience. Remember: The audience only gets what you give them.

Get A Second Opinion

Another important editing technique is to get someone else's opinion, because it is so difficult to remain objective about something so personal. A trusted advisor, colleague, friend or family member is a good choice. Just be sure the person has a good ear for evaluating presentations and speeches, and has heard a fair number of them. It makes no sense to ask someone for a critique who hasn't the faintest idea what a good presentation sounds like. Also, whomever you choose must not be afraid to critique the presentation, so subordinates may be out, no matter what you say ahead of time about being eager to hear constructive criticism. Finally, keep in mind that the final decisions on what to keep and what to throw out are always yours. Don't let yourself be bullied.

Video Requires Special Editing Discipline

When doing videos (Speakret #16), people often make the big mistake of going on for too long. Think of your videos as TV commercials. When I started doing TV commercial jingles, it was common to do 60-second jingles. Then, 30-second jingles became the fashion. Today, it's 10 or 15-seconds. In fact, when you see the rare 30 or 60-second commercial these days, it feels like forever! And that's what all your viewers are feeling, too.

So, keep your videos very short. 30-45 seconds is plenty of time to deliver your message. Keep that up for awhile. I currently have hundreds of videos on my YouTube channel and with few exceptions (vlogs, tutorials) they are very short, with many less than a minute and most under 5. As you gain a following, people will stick with you longer.

Today, the trend is toward short, content-rich communication and presentations. People are busy. Show them you get that.

SPEAKRETS® TOOLKIT

We speak at an average of about 140 words per minute (wpm).* The following chart contains some guidelines...

Minutes of speech	Number of words
1	140
5	700
10	1400
15	2100
20	2800
30	4200

*This is an average only and thus, these numbers are approximate. Some people will speak at a slower average rate, and some faster.

SPEAKRETS®

SPEAKRET #29: Sleep Well By Anticipating Questions and Objections

-Ruth's Truth-

Be ready to address all questions, and especially "Nightmare Questions."

There is a part of the speaker/communicator's stock in trade that too many people are unprepared for: Questions and objections. Depending on the type of presentation, these can start right from the beginning, occur during breaks you dictate, or wait until the end.

One thing that any presenter should do before a presentation is to anticipate questions and objections. Here is a prime opportunity to get colleagues, your manager, or an event organizer involved. If you put your heads together, you can usually anticipate almost every question or objection that is likely to be raised. As you might imagine, being prepared in this way will reduce the number of unpleasant surprises, help you maintain control, and identify you as confident, knowledgeable, and prepared.

Managing Media Questions

Most of the media training I do with celebrities and public figures involves scoping out all the possible questions the press might ask and, as you might imagine, they can ask some doozies! They always are trying to get the big scoop, find out something about a famous person that hasn't been revealed before, and publish it before the competition does. The celebs are under intense scrutiny and it's very stressful. That's when they call me.

Before I go in to work with someone, I do my homework, typically asking for any and all relevant press that's been done to date. I'll also need to see the film or TV show or any other project they may be working on. I have to admit, it's a lot of fun to be paid to go to the movies, especially when you get to sit in a plush, private screening room.

When I meet with the client, the work includes going through all the questions. There can be 40 or 50 that I come up with. The first round is the practice round: I ask the question, the client tries to answer, I suggest ways to answer. The second round is the "dress rehearsal." We go through the questions and hit all the tough spots. They're a lot more comfortable by now. Subsequently we do Media 101, which includes all the techniques they can use to maintain control of the interview. One area we spend a good deal of time is how to deflect personal questions. My advice is always the same: Your personal life is private, so don't succumb to the pressure to answer. There are techniques involved here that enable them to avoid answering these questions in a comfortable way. The reason for this caution is if you open the door, even a little, journalists will barge right in.

When it's over, I write a 10+ page comprehensive summary containing everything we worked on. They're free then to review, take it with them, and refer to it as they need to. They love this feature. See? Movie stars need notes, too!

The lesson here is my non-famous clients are not that different from the famous ones. These are professional performers and still they have trouble. They have to work at it. And so do you. The next time you receive an opportunity to be covered in the press, do your homework. Sit down and just write down every question you can think of and answer them as if you were in the actual studio or, if it's a print interview, on the phone with the reporter.

By the way, never say anything you don't want to see in print. Nothing is ever off the record.

Don't Forget Nightmare Questions

The most important questions to write down are what I call "nightmare questions." Interestingly, when we're preparing for a media appearance, we imagine it will all go swimmingly. It's akin to my advice around rehearsal meaning saying it out loud because we're all very eloquent in our own heads (Speakret #5). It's human nature to want to avoid difficulty and anticipating the "holes" or weaknesses in your story or position, or where objections or challenges might be raised causes discomfort. For that reason alone, I caution clients to think whether they'd rather display that discomfort in the privacy of their office or on national TV?

Open Questions Quell Resistance

Outside the media spotlight, there times when listeners create resistance. Try to get to the bottom of the resistance by probing and asking open questions. Open questions require more than a yes or no answer and get the person on the receiving end to do the talking.

SPEAKRETS® TOOLKIT

Open questions usually begin with the following words:

What...

Why...

How...

Tell me more...

Can you describe…

Another technique is called "checking." Check with your listeners periodically by asking questions such as

How does that sound?

Does this meet your needs?

Are we on the right track?

Also, bear in mind the following guidelines:

1. **No matter what you hear, you must never, ever become defensive.** Remain calm. Remind yourself: The person who is giving you a hard time might be just having a bad day.

2. **When in doubt, listen.** The person may have information about your subject that has not yet been revealed to you.

3. **Don't contradict or argue.** (Don't automatically agree either!)

4. **If you don't have the answer, say so.** Then promise to get back with the answer by a specific date and time.

5. **Show your interest in solving the problem; display concern, empathy.**

6. **Maintain absolute political correctness.** Do not use bad language or questionable humor.

7. **Make good eye contact especially when receiving challenges to your information or criticism.**

8. **Project confidence, even if you don't feel it.** Look at objections as opportunities to negotiate.

Anticipate "Nightmare Questions:"

1. What is the one question you are most worried about?

2. What are 2-3 other questions that concern you?

3. Why would you like to avoid these questions?

4. Is there any question you have had difficulty answering in the past?

5. What topic has the most potential to do damage to you or the organization?

SPEAKRET #30: Merge Your Style With Technique

-Ruth's Truth-

Successful speaking and communicating, at their core, are all about personal style combined with carefully honed technique.

Everyone wants to know about personal style. So what, exactly, is personal style when it comes to speaking and communicating? And how do you integrate it with technique?

Basically, personal style means all the aspects of your personality, the specialized procedures you and you alone use to deliver your message, and all the personal decisions you make to put on a great show. We're all unique and, therefore, so are our personal styles. We all start naturally differentiated from each other and we should make the most of that.

Technique is something else. First and foremost, technique is a series of best practices that have evolved over time, but have, in large part, remained the same. For instance, we know it is a best practice to prepare (Speakret #5). Another best practice is to be physically and vocally animated and engaging (Speakret #26). This entire book of Speakrets® has been one, big treatise on sharpening technique.

Style v. Technique

People are always afraid of sacrificing their style in service of technique. They equate style with who they are and fear losing part of themselves, or coming across as phony or inauthentic (Speakret #2). Mostly this is about dealing with some mistaken, but closely held beliefs and ingrained habits of speaking and communicating that are hard to break. Change feels very uncomfortable. For example, when I direct a client who doesn't know what to do with her hands to use them naturally, hold them a certain way, or choreograph a particular gesture, she always tells me it feels awful and unnatural. My response...

> "I don't care how you feel. I only care
> how you look and sound."

I know that after a time, the gesturing will become integrated, feel more natural, and get results in the form of better presentations that influence decision-makers, the people in charge of raises, promotions, assignments, clients, business. And that feels pretty good!

Script, Notes, Or Memorize?

One of the biggest issues having to do with style, and one my clients constantly struggle with, is whether to script out a speech and read it to an audience verbatim, to use notes of some type, or to memorize the speech whole. The most successful, engaging speakers really know their presentations, although they're not completely memorized. They have practiced enough times so that they know what's coming next. They may not say it the same way twice, but they do have the presentation down so whatever way the words come out, it works.

Handling Notes

Notes vary in form ranging from an outline on a sheet of paper to index cards to floor monitors (known in the business as "confidence monitors"). Slides can also serve as notes, and would seem to be a good choice. But as I write in Speakret #24, it is quite difficult to produce interesting, effective slides for most business people and my recommendation is to stay as far away from slides as possible.

I always use notes – as in 100% of the time – which surprises many people. Notes do not detract from my effectiveness as a speaker and they provide a great safety net. When I'm speaking, I either set the notes down on a nearby stand that I can return to if I need a memory jog (podiums are great for this), or I hold the notes so I can glance down at them easily. They become an extension of my hand. If I'm particularly animated, both hands are in action and my notes just happen to be in one of them. I also love the confidence monitor.

In fact, the next time you go to an industry conference, watch how some of the main stage speakers subtly glance down. There are monitors that contain their notes placed strategically along the stage's apron. They've practiced, of course, so they look confident and in control. The notes provide that safety net and the monitors enable them to depart from the podium. As I alluded to earlier, notes are not meant to substitute for truly learning and internalizing your presentation so if they weren't available, you could deliver it successfully anyway.

Reading From A Script is Very Risky

What about all the speakers who read from prepared scripts? I find them to be almost universally unsuccessful. The writing is often poor and stilted. In addition, the text keeps the speaker glued to the page and to the podium, which interferes terribly with their communication with listeners.

I have had many occasions to work with speakers working from teleprompters. This, of course, creates the illusion that the speaker is looking at the audience. It still requires specialty writing by a very skilled speechwriter. And it still compels the speaker to stand in one spot.

I bring us back to President Obama, who has made using a teleprompter part of his brand. Over and over again, we see the President standing behind that podium, delivering scripted remarks and, while early on, he was successful, he has since settled into a flatter, sing-song pattern, exacerbated by his scanning back and forth between each reflector (the glass panes on either side of the podium that are showing the scrolling speech). I even have a name for this: Wimbledon. With few exceptions, his recent speeches have been unsuccessful as a result. The bloom is off the rose (and the opposition never lets him forget it).

Please Don't Use a Podium

A podium places a barrier between you and your audience. It's a crutch. It's made for people 6 feet and taller. I've already described other, better ways to stay on track. The podium is a good place to rest your notes that you can return to if you need a memory jog. If you're reluctant to give it up entirely, just step out to the side so it isn't blocking you. But my strong recommendation is take center stage and own it! (Speakret #15.)

There is so much to think about when communicating and speaking...

- *Do my words resonate?*

- *Am I moving my hands naturally?*

- *Can they hear me in the last row?*

- *Am I being persuasive?*

The list goes on.

Merging your personal style with technique can be frustrating and confusing. You will want to give up, leave good (or bad) enough alone and tell yourself it's not that important. But it is. Don't let go of that thought as you persevere.

It gets easier.

Following are three general examples of personal style that most of us fit into, followed by suggestions for adding and integrating technique so that it doesn't all feel so foreign. It will take time, so be patient.

SPEAKRETS® TOOLKIT
Quiet, Introverted, or Shy

To the quiet, introverted, or shy (and I know these are different from each other), integrating our personal style with technique that will get us noticed can seem like climbing Mt. Everest. After all, how can you be expected to get up on a stage and act all outgoing, when inside you're thinking, *"just get me out of here"*?
Here's how:

1. Remember this is just another self – your presentation and communication self. You already have many different selves that you adapt to specific occasions and environments. This is no different (Speakret #2).

2. Closely observe your non-verbals during informal communication during which you feel comfortable. I guarantee that you're moving your hands, body, and voice in ways that are natural and that make your words rich in meaning.

3. From your observations, take one of the nonverbal codes (voice, gestures, posture, stance, eyes) and transfer it to the workplace platform. Work on that code, and only that code, for a couple of weeks until it starts to feel more comfortable.

4. Add another and then another until you have integrated them with your personal style.

Cerebral

The cerebral personal style is information and data driven. Engineers, technology professionals, doctors, accountants, lawyers, financial professionals, and others in professions where it's all about the numbers, the science, or the research tend to communicate as if that is all that matters. You have to help the medicine go down and here are some ways to achieve that …

1. When you go to conferences and industry gatherings, closely observe the technique of speakers that engage you. Identify and jot down what they do that makes them engaging. Notice how it enhances their ability to communicate their message.

2. Try some of these engaging behaviors out on the your own, smaller stage. Perhaps it's adding more vocal variety (Speakret #8) or getting out from behind the podium (Speakret #30).

3. Since cerebral people are data people, keep a log, writing down exactly how it feels to try out the new behavior and the outcome. Ask trusted colleagues who observe you what they think and write that down, too.

4. Over time, review your log and notice how your improvements have evolved. Adjust or discard the behaviors that haven't worked and increase your effort on behalf of the ones that have.

Extroverted

You may think extroverts have no work to do, but, in fact, they do and it's not what you think. Chances are they don't have to tone things down. Extroverts, however, often get so excited about what they are saying, they forget about their audience. Here are some ways to hone technique so the extroversion doesn't obscure the message...

1. Remember WIIFM at all times (What's In It For Me). Make sure your content is completely focused on the needs of your audience, which is not how excited you are about it. Exciting them by the way you deliver it is.

2. Read the room. If you see people are distracted by your non-verbals, it may be time to adjust and adapt. You will not always be in front of fellow extroverts. Remember your introverted and cerebral colleagues.

3. Don't pace the stage or move in a jittery or jerky way. Plant yourself and move purposefully. Use pauses and silences liberally to give yourself –

and your audience – a break. Extroverts usually have a lot of pent up energy and run the risk of exhausting their audiences. Don't do that!

IT'S A WRAP...

There you have it. Thirty Speakrets®. Thirty opportunities to learn, grow, and improve. Make the most of them!

Now that you know what to work on, practice, and review, you've got every reason to go out and volunteer to speak, to meet with clients and customers face-to-face, to communicate in a thoughtful, measured, and powerful way. Doing so will help you move from theory into practice (remember, it is on-the-job-training), and will also give you a remarkable differentiator in your career.

Why? Because most people don't know how to do it, are too afraid to try it, or reject it. They've never had any coaching, or are filled with dread, or, dumbest of all, dismiss these skills as "soft" instead of accepting them as the essential, professional skills they are. Everyone who feels that way is now a step behind you. Take advantage of that.

So... now it's on you. Seek out the new venues where you can get out and practice what you have learned here. Then let me know how things are going. I mean it! Visit me at www.ruthsherman.com. Follow me on Twitter, Facebook, LinkedIn, and YouTube – I'll respond!

The Speakrets® + Ruth's Truths

I. Private Speakrets®

SPEAKRET #1: Listen
Ruth's Truth: Listening is the most important – and most neglected – of all the persuasion and communication skills.

SPEAKRET #2: Be Your Best Self
Ruth's Truth: Instead of striving for "authenticity," become the best, true version of yourself in each unique situation to captivate and touch people.

SPEAKRET #3: Shatter The Charisma Myth
Ruth's Truth: Charisma isn't inborn. It's <u>learned.</u>

SPEAKRET #4: Watch What You Say Because Words CAN Hurt
Ruth's Truth: Calibrate your communication with the twin goals of being clear and direct, while causing the least offense.

SPEAKRET #5: Do Your Homework
Ruth's Truth: Preparation is the magic bullet to successful communication and presentation – and the single biggest obstacle.

SPEAKRET #6: Your Attire Speaks Volumes
Ruth's Truth: Dress and adornment – all the sartorial choices we make – communicate a strong message before a word is uttered.

SPEAKRET #7: Emblems Display Our Status
Ruth's Truth: The public evaluates us by things we use to decorate ourselves.

SPEAKRET #8: Seduce With Your Voice
Ruth's Truth: A beautiful speaking voice coupled with precise diction is like a fingerprint, a unique differentiator.

SPEAKRET #9: Name-Calling Is An Art
Ruth's Truth: Foster good will by at least attempting to correctly pronounce an unfamiliar or foreign name.

SPEAKRET #10: Know When To Say "Sorry!"
Ruth's Truth: Apology and expressions of regret are powerful communication tools that will defuse any conflict.

II. Business Speakrets®

SPEAKRET #11: Know Your Audience
Ruth's Truth: If you don't know your audience, you won't be able to give them what they came for.

SPEAKRET #12: Be A Super-Connector

Ruth' Truth: Introduce people to each other imaginatively and actively. You will be appreciated and remembered.

SPEAKRET #13: Persuasive Language – Take A Page From The Pols

Ruth's Truth: Words, carefully selected, can change hearts and minds.

SPEAKRET #14: Cultivate A Tribe of Die-Hard Fans

Ruth's Truth: Instead of creating customers, whom you must chase, create fans, who will chase you.

SPEAKRET #15: Be Excited And Passionate Like Steve Jobs

Ruth's Truth: Excitement and passion are contagious. Steve Jobs built an empire with this simple knowledge.

SPEAKRET #16: Join The Video Revolution

Ruth's Truth: Learn on-camera presence, a.k.a., VideoCharisma®, or be left behind.

Speakret #17: Harness The Enormous Power Of Symbolism

Ruth's Truth: Symbols have great meaning. Deploy them with care.

Speakret #18: Become A Media Darling

Ruth's Truth: Becoming a media darling is all about reputation management.

Speakret #19: Face-To-Face Is Still King

Ruth's Truth: When it comes to communication, face-to-face is primary. Always has been, always will be.

SPEAKRET #20: Appreciate Wallflower Power

Ruth's Truth: Being shy is no reason to stay out of the spotlight.

III. Public Speakrets®

SPEAKRET #21: Master The Platform

Ruth's Truth: Polished, confident presentation skills are unsurpassed methods of increasing your personal and professional impact.

SPEAKRET #22: Get Emotional

Ruth's Truth: Strategically deploy emotions to connect and be relatable.

Speakret #23: Find The Best Stories

Ruth's Truth: Stories make otherwise dry and boring information come alive.

SPEAKRET #24: Stop Using Slides

Ruth's Truth: Try to rid yourself of slides. If you must use them, however, use very few, make them bold, graphic, and easy to read.

Speakret #25: Channel The Power Of Stage Fright

Ruth's Truth: Stage Fright goes with the territory. It can help you be amazing so don't fight it – use it.

Speakret #26: Crack The Nonverbal Codes

Ruth's Truth: Nonverbal communication gives meaning to our words and makes us believable.

Speakret #27: Let Your Hands Do Some Talking

Ruth's Truth: Gestures enrich our words and help us think.

Speakret #28: Keep It Short, Keep Their Attention

Ruth's Truth: No one ever objects to a short presentation.

SPEAKRET #29: Sleep Well By Anticipating Questions And Objections

Ruth's Truth: Be ready to address all questions, and especially "Nightmare Questions."

Speakret #30: Merge Your Style With Technique

Ruth's Truth: Speaking and communicating, at their core, are all about personal style combined with carefully honed technique.

SPEAKRETS®

About Ruth Sherman (Official Boring Bio)

Ruth Sherman, M.A., is a strategic communications consultant focusing on preparing business leaders, celebrities and public figures, politicians, and entrepreneurs to leverage critical public communication opportunities including the development and delivery of keynote speeches, webcasts, investor presentations, road shows, awards presentations, political campaigns, media contact, and video. Her clients hail from the A-list of international business, entertainment and fashion, including Apple, JP Morgan, Timex, Deloitte, Universal/Focus Features, Paramount, Versace International, and many other major companies that cannot be mentioned. Three of her clients have won Oscars and one the Pulitzer Prize.

As a speaker, Ruth is highly sought after and has addressed many associations including the Association for Talent Development (ATD, formerly ASTD) National Conference and Expo, Insurance Conference Planners

Association (ICPA), National Investor Relations Institute (NIRI) and the National Speakers Association (NSA National Conferences).

She is regularly contacted by the press and has been featured in the New York Times, Washington Post, National Journal, New York Post, Wall Street Journal, Miami Herald, San Francisco Chronicle, on ABC, CBS, MSNBC, CNBC, FOX, the BBC and NY1 where she was a recurring commentator on the communication skills of the participants on the TV show, *The Apprentice*, starring Donald Trump.

Ruth is a former Fast Company Magazine "Expert Blogger" where her columns on leadership communication are posted.

As a leading authority on political communication, Ruth comments extensively on elections, focusing on candidates' communication skills and arguing that these skills can make or break a race. As a former faculty member of the Women's Campaign School at Yale

University, she has addressed and coached hundreds of candidates running for office.

Ruth began her professional life as a performer in New York, focusing on commercial singing and announcing. As one of a handful of successful jingle-singers, her voice was heard around the world on commercials for such clients as Coca-Cola, Ford, Michelob and Clairol. After receiving a master's degree in speech and interpersonal communication from New York University, where she also taught for several years in NYU's School of Education, she opened her consulting and speaking business.

Ruth Sherman is the author of the McGraw-Hill book; **Get Them To See It Your Way, Right Away: How To Persuade Anyone Of Anything**. It was designated a "Best Business Book" by the prestigious Library Journal and translated into Chinese and Romanian.

Ruth Sherman lives in Connecticut with her husband, Brad Olsen-Ecker and Orderv, the cockatiel (first one's name was Cocktail; next one's will likely be Entrée or, maybe, Dessert). Their older daughter, Britt, is an actress, singer, and photographer in Baltimore and their younger daughter, Lily, is a recent graduate of The Pratt Institute having majored in metal sculpture.

About me... (Unofficial, Fun Bio)

I work with CEOs, Celebrities and Small Business Entrepreneurs to help them become great speakers, presenters and media darlings so they can reach many more clients faster, and get more business. My current top interest is Video, in particular, on-camera presence, and its powerful intersection with Social Media.

I've had the honor of working with some of the world's largest and most prestigious companies, top CEOs, movie stars and international celebrities. Five of my clients have won Oscars and one, the Pulitzer Prize!

But you don't have to be famous to work with me!

Here are 10 things you may not know about me:

1. I'm a political junkie.

2. I cannot resist coffee ice cream.

3. I cry every time I watch the ending of "ET" and during the Broadway Musical overtures.

4. I have a terrible potty mouth.

5. I love to sing opera (still have my high C), and listen to select sopranos, but not to watch operas.

6. I love the theatre too much to ever be able to move too far from New York, which bothers me.

7. I was one of the singers on the famous Coca-Cola jingle, "I'd Like To Teach The World To Sing in Perfect Harmony" (but not the first round in the 70s because I'm much younger than those people).

8. I'm no lady. And I think that's a good thing.

9. I consider myself a vegan, but slip regularly (see #2), so who am I kidding?

10. I believe communication can change the world.

I've been an Expert Blogger for Fast Company where I get to write about how communication impacts relationships and leadership. You can read my stuff at http://www.fastcompany.com/user/ruth-sherman.

I'm a leading authority on Political Communication, widely quoted in the press on the topic and can state with utter confidence that he or she who communicates best, wins!

My first book, **"Get Them to See It Your Way, Right Away: How To Persuade Anyone Of Anything,"** (McGraw-Hill) has been translated into Chinese and Romanian (?) and also named a Library Journal "Best Business Book."

I have an M.A. in Speech and Interpersonal Communication from NYU, but everything I do work-wise is really a result of what I learned in my performing arts training (bachelor of music) and as a professional singer and actress, my first career.

I have offices in Greenwich, CT and Los Angeles, CA, but spend most of my time in CT with my husband (and resident humorist & designer) Brad Olsen-Ecker, and Orderv, the cockatiel. (First one's name was Cocktail;

next one will either be Entrée or Dessert.) Our older daughter, Britt, is an actress, singer, and photographer in Baltimore and our younger daughter, Lily, a recent graduate of The Pratt Institute, having majored in metal sculpture.

www.RuthSherman.com

48302314R00137

Made in the USA
Middletown, DE
15 September 2017